I'm afraid that serious, humor... ...on't immediately think the... ...y need... ...be wrong. This book breath...es fresh air into stale, windowless lives ever committed to hustle and hard work. With warm and witty storytelling, Courtney Ellis lead us into the good news of the kingdom—that it's a playful, joyful place. What a gift her words are, especially for dark and difficult days.

JEN POLLOCK MICHEL,
award-winning author of *Surprised by Paradox*
and *A Habit Called Faith.*

Courtney Ellis offers a rare, timely combination of sound theology, personal transparency, accessible style, and sharp wit. The world needs more writers like Courtney, and readers need more books by her.

KAREN SWALLOW PRIOR,
author of *On Reading Well: Finding the Good Life*
through *Great Books*

My wife Maile and I are always talking about how important whimsy and playfulness are when it comes to writing and creativity, so when I saw the subtitle of Ellis's book, I couldn't help but smile: *Let playfulness lift your load and renew your spirit?* Yes, please. As a firstborn child who holds seriousness in high regard, I need the freeing and joyful message, and playful applications, this book has to offer. But don't we all? Seriousness has taken over our lives in the form of somber religion, stern politics, and pessimistic outlooks. Ellis's book arrives at just the right time, and her kind and easygoing voice makes this book a joy to read, the first step on the road to a more creative, whimsical, and playful life.

SHAWN SMUCKER,
author of *The Weight of Memory*

This isn't a book to read for mere intellectual satisfaction. It is a book whose principles I plan to further incorporate into my own life and into the life of my family. Let us follow in Courtney's footsteps as she follows in Jesus's footsteps.

MARLENA GRAVES,
author of *The Way Up is Down: Becoming*
Yourself by Forgetting Yourself

Great news: you don't have to abandon your responsible, grown-up self in order to invite playfulness back into your life! Fun, curiosity, and wonder are absolutely essential to our well-being, and Courtney Ellis has written the step-by-step guide to experiencing more of all three, right where you are, every day.

MELISSA CAMARA WILKINS,
author of *Permission Granted: Be Who You Were*
Made to Be and Let Go of the Rest

Jesus said that the way of faith is becoming like a child, and in *Happy Now* Courtney Ellis shows us how. Through honesty, wisdom, and humor, Ellis invites us to practice the healing, renewing posture of playfulness. Maybe faith actually was always meant to include fun.

K. J. RAMSEY,
licensed professional counselor and author of *This Too*
Shall Last: Finding Grace When Suffering Lingers

This book is brilliant! Deep, light, entertaining and practical. It is truly an invitation into a more joyful and God-filled way of life.

ANNA WOOFENDEN,
author of *This is God's Table*

Once again, Courtney Ellis's pastoral care and deep wisdom is woven throughout her writing in such a way that invites us to navigate life with intention and care, to not bypass the heaviness of life, and to remember the value of playfulness in our lives. What a timely gift *Happy Now* is as a gentle reminder to reconnect with the practice of play!

HOLLY K. OXHANDLER, PhD, LMSW,
Associate Dean for Research & Faculty Development, Garland School of Social Work, Baylor University

With *Happy Now*, Courtney Ellis demonstrates that taking God seriously means embracing the possibility for delight—and sheer fun—he placed in our hearts. Absorbing this wonderful book, I kept asking how the church might look and live if we believed Ellis's words. What if they knew we were Christians by our play? Read on and catch the vision.

AARIK DANIELSEN,
***Fathom Magazine* columnist**

Can you imagine God playing? What about dancing, singing, and laughing—with you? During times of suffering, we need God's smile more than ever. Faithful, encouraging, hilarious, and heartfelt, *Happy Now* reminds you that playfulness can be holiness.

CATHERINE MCNIEL,
author of *All Shall Be Well*

A witty and wise guide, Courtney Ellis urges us to consider the positive influence of play on our mental, emotional, and spiritual health. With self-deprecating humor, she artfully welcomes those of us paralyzed by seriousness to embrace whimsy and delight.

LESLIE VERNER,
author of *Invited: The Power of Hospitality in an Age of Loneliness*

Courtney has the gift of taking subjects in which I don't naturally excel (motherhood, uncluttering, playing) and showing me how to do them both *on* purpose and *with* purpose. *Happy Now* is a field guide for the journey of learning to play, written by a funny friend who keeps it real while maintaining a pastor's focus of what actually *is* real. God wants us to enjoy our lives, and Courtney gives us a thoughtful exploration of how to do so.

REBECCA COCHRAN,
cohost of the Woven podcast

Courtney has done it again! In her third book, she returns with her combination of humor and humility, to share with her readers a personal struggle, how she overcame it with God's help while at the same time making a very personal struggle relatable to everyone whether they are in her same boat or not. As someone who struggles with productivity over playfulness, I'm thankful for Courtney's gentle encouragement and practical advice on how to renew my spirit through play.

REBECCA PEET,
cohost of the Woven podcast, certified Enneagram coach

Happy Now is a gorgeous, imaginative, and liberating reminder that God is not only concerned with our holiness but with our enjoyment of him and his good gifts. Courtney demonstrates how playfulness enriches our soul, mind, body, and spirit.

ALICIA AKINS,
author of *Invitations to Abundance*

Courtney Ellis does it again! *Happy Now* is equal parts hilarity, honesty and holy invitation. Her antics at a twenty-two-dollar spin class will make you cringe and laugh out loud at the same time— after all, Ellis relishes in making real the everyday messiness and joy of her life, while simultaneously daring the reader to join the God of playfulness in the greatest "yes ... and" of all.

CARA MEREDITH,
author of *The Color of Life*

With humor and grace Courtney Ellis reminds us in *Happy Now* that God uses playfulness in our lives to enrich our faith in Christ and deepen our relationships with others.

KRISTINE ARAGON BRUCE,
Associate Pastor of First Presbyterian Church of Grand Haven

Happy Now is a delightful exploration of the transformative power of playfulness. Courtney's accessible invitations give permission to have fun, get silly, and enter into the abundant freedom God desires for you.

STEPHANIE JENKINS,
Author of *Field Guides for the Way*

Once again, Courtney Ellis has yanked back the curtain we so often erect between the sacred and mundane. With a spirit of whimsy, she beckons the reader to join her on an adventure of playfulness, insisting that God is present in the giggles and gaffes. Ellis serves as a trusted guide on the road to happiness, accompanying the reader through the intersections of Scripture, psychology, and humor. If you are weary and worn, *Happy Now* will lead you to the One who restores and refreshes through the gift of play.

STEPHANIE LOBDELL,
author of *Signs of Life: Resurrecting Hope out of Ordinary Losses*

Happy Now offers a much-needed deep breath of fresh air and light. Whatever extraordinary challenges you have faced in the past two years—illness or financial crisis, loss of a loved one or a clinical anxiety diagnosis—introducing playfulness into your life is bound to be soul medicine of the best, most accessible kind. Let Courtney coach you into a life space punctuated by moments of joy rather than stress and exhaustion, inspired by the playful God who created us in his own image. In order to thrive in our overly serious culture, creating a lifestyle of playfulness is not just a nicety—it's a requirement.

HARMONY HARKEMA,
writer, editor, speaker and writing coach

For my parents—
two of the most playful people I know.

Dad, I'll never forget coasting on fumes into that gas station in rural Wyoming in a fifteen-passenger prison van filled with the entire church youth group. Your stories were so hilarious that all the responsible adults forgot to check the gauge.

Mom, I still can't believe you walked backward off that cliff. Wait, yes I can. Because you're that awesome.

Contents

Foreword

All sorts of people were attracted to Jesus, including children. That certainly wouldn't have been because Jesus was standoffish, overly serious, mean, or crotchety! There is a lightness, a joviality, a playfulness to the one who created each of us. How could God not be playful, given the hilarity and complexity of human beings and the intriguing plant and animal kingdoms? Playfulness and fun are integral to who God is.

Courtney Ellis piqued my interest when she revealed she was writing a book about playfulness. She tells us: "Despite living in one of the wealthiest countries on earth, Americans are among the most anxious people on the planet."

"Relentless seriousness," as she puts it, "is wearing us all down." Indeed it is.

And herein is the crux of Courtney's wisdom in *Happy Now*—she writes, "The paradox of play is this: it is not because life is easy that we engage in whimsy, but because life is difficult." Some of us cannot think of the last time we were truly playful. We're too busy, occupied with making a living or caring for others. The cares of this world are wearing us down. But as Courtney demonstrates, it is precisely *because* of these things that we have to cultivate playfulness. It need not cost money or too much effort, even. But it might require intention until it becomes natural.

This isn't a book to read for mere intellectual satisfaction. It is a book with principles I plan to further incorporate into my own life and into the life of my family—even into my church's life. Courtney offers us lots of ideas throughout the book while playfully weaving in and out anecdotes from her own life, Jesus' life, research, and theology. Some of my favorite suggestions have to do with improv groups and block parties. But lest you read that and be immediately overwhelmed at the mere thought of either, take heart. Courtney encourages us to start small. Nurturing a spirit of playfulness can be as easy as smiling at a stranger in the grocery store.

Playfulness is good for our souls, essential for our personal and cultural health. It is a spiritual discipline that needs to be promoted in our lives and churches, lest we become too serious for Jesus. So let us emulate our Lord by incorporating whimsy and play into our lives! Let us follow in Courtney's footsteps as she follows in Jesus' footsteps.

(And here's to hoping she gets published in *The New York Times*!)

MARLENA GRAVES
Author, *The Way Up Is Down: Finding Yourself by Forgetting Yourself*
August 2020

A Note

I wrote *Happy Now* during a uniquely difficult time, finishing the first draft two weeks before Covid-19 shutdowns began. All descriptions of indoor gatherings, crowded events, and large group worship illustrate events that took place before Covid-19 entered the global consciousness. While I revised portions of this book to reflect the temporary new realities created by this pandemic, I've left other segments intact to serve as a witness to what was and a hope of what will someday again be.

This book also contains a great deal of autobiographical material. All dialogue, events, dates, and descriptions are reconstructed to the best of my research and recollection. A few have been condensed. While my memory is certainly fallible, I have done my sincere best to stay true to the spirit and timeline of each interaction. At various points, names or details have been changed to protect the privacy of a particular person, and when this is the case, such changes are noted.

Finally, I've thanked God every day that this book project came to me when it did, because without the lessons of playfulness, I don't know how our little family would have weathered all the macro- and micro-griefs this season wrought. Play and Jesus got us through.

Play and Jesus will help us—and you—heal.

Suddenly I understand that I am happy.
—JANE KENYON, "THE SUITOR"

PART I

A Playful Solution to a Serious Problem

1

The Playfulness Key

A joyful heart is good medicine.
—PROVERBS 17:22

You are nine years old, sitting at a desk in an elementary school classroom. It is hot and stuffy. The tag in your shirt scratches at the back of your neck. The teacher drones on about a subject that holds no interest to you—fractions, adverbs, the War of 1812—and her tone tells you that she isn't very interested, either. The minute hand on the clock above her head seems frozen in place. You yawn. You sigh. You shift in your chair.

Then it happens.

A paper airplane sails over the heads of your classmates, dipping gracefully at the front of the room before falling to the tiled floor, and sliding, with a soft hiss, to a stop.

The teacher pauses, mid-sentence. You hold your breath. Her eyes scan the room and her brow furrows. You and your classmates are completely silent. Then the teacher breaks into a smile.

"Well," she says, "now that I have your attention, let's turn to page forty-two." The class chuckles and dutifully opens their textbooks.

As you turn the pages, you realize that something has shifted. Suddenly, you are different. Lighter. Freer.

Happier.

Though your circumstances haven't changed, you have.

If you picked up this book because you long for happiness but aren't quite sure how to find it, let me invite you into an uplifting journey on the surest breeze I know: the power of *playfulness*.

Like a paper airplane sailing above a classroom, playfulness raises us from our doldrums, lifts our gazes, and buoys our spirits. It holds the power to transform our lives. A gift from the God who created us, playfulness reminds us that we are a people dearly loved and set free to tell everyone that they are dearly loved, too.

While the influence of play can scarcely be overstated, its importance is commonly overlooked. We are often far too focused on completing the necessary tasks of life to spend time pursuing frivolity. Put another way: who has time to play when the challenges facing us are so very, very serious?

That, my friends, is the question we will tackle together in the pages ahead.

And we must tackle it because, as Thomas Hobbes famously wrote, life can be "solitary, poor, nasty, brutish, and short."[1] Scripture describes our lives as fading as quickly as "the flowers of the field."[2] We don't have much time here on this earth, and the time we do have overflows with obstacles, tedium, and heartache. The paradox of play is this: we engage in whimsy not because life is easy, but because life is difficult.

A brief example, if I may. In the early 1980s, my grandfather was diagnosed with a brain tumor. The surgeons told my grandparents that they were confident in their skill, but it was still brain surgery (in the early 80s!) and not without risk. Still, if he didn't have the procedure, he would lose his eyesight. The night before he went under the knife, his nurses were surprised to hear music coming from his hospital room. His four adult children had driven from far and wide and gathered with their mother by his bedside. Instead of worrying or weeping, they were singing hymns.

Were they nervous? Of course. But on the eve of what could be their last morning together, they chose to express their love through play. There were tears, but there was also the joy of voices lifted together—the very same voices that had been blending since my grandparents first set their tots around the piano decades earlier. (Lest you think it was pure idyll, these same voices also argued over who was encroaching on whose vocal part—yes, even on the eve of a brain surgery. Turns out a little good-natured sibling bickering is just one more way to play.)

My grandfather has always espoused the words of one of my favorite hymns:

> *Heart of my own heart, whatever befall*
> *Still be my vision, O ruler of all.*[3]

I wasn't at that bedside; I hadn't even been born yet. But the story has echoed down through our family for decades and changed the way we live, even on the cusp of potential tragedy.

I'm not saying that playfulness will cure all that ails you. Laughter may be the best medicine, but it certainly isn't the only one we need. Stay in your small group. Keep your therapist. Continue to take the medication you've been prescribed. Playfulness isn't a one-stop solution to trauma, anxiety, or depression. It won't set a broken leg, get you through college, or magically transform an ailing marriage. There are times we will each need a medical expert, require a change in habits, or benefit from talking to someone. This book is not meant to substitute for any of these good and helpful things.

But I also believe there is almost nothing that playfulness cannot make a little bit better, a little bit easier, and a whole lot more fun.

And that, my friends, is worth a lot. A whole lot.

Onward.

Whimsy Defined

Playfulness begins with a first, simple yes. When a smile is offered, do you smile in return? When music plays, will you dance? When the ball is thrown, do you hold out your hand to catch it? Playfulness follows a simple pattern of *invitation*, *permission*, and *release*: We are invited into play (or we invite ourselves). We receive permission to play (or we grant ourselves permission). Finally, there is the release of falling into playfulness—the moment of joy itself. This pattern takes place all over, from Broadway theaters to kitchen tables, from college classrooms to apartment balconies, from nursery schools to assisted living facilities. It is visible in every human age group, culture, and society, as well as the higher tiers of the animal kingdom. Otters, anyone? Dolphins? Dachshunds? According to play expert Stuart Brown, the more advanced the species, the more it plays.[4]

Playfulness is good-natured and a little mischievous. It lives with open hands, not worried about controlling each little detail, but instead available for spontaneity and discovery. Improvisation is playful; so is wonder. Playfulness helps us embrace even mistakes and failure as opportunities. (Think of painter Bob Ross's "happy accidents," where a misplaced glob of paint suddenly turns into a lovely pine tree, adding just the right touch to a landscape.) It is a way of moving about in the world ready to be surprised, excited, enthralled, and blessed. Playfulness is key to understanding ourselves and the God who created us, and key to living into the freedom God gives to us in Christ. (More on that soon.)

I use *playfulness* rather than *play* because we tend to think of play as a limited activity. *Play* can seem binary—we are either playing or we are not—but it's possible for *playfulness* to infuse nearly every minute and area of our lives. We can playfully wash the dishes, even if few of us would describe that activity itself as *play*. It's possible to be playful in our relationships, our work, our recreation. We can keep a house playfully and raise children playfully. We can run a meeting playfully, sew a button playfully, and shop for groceries playfully. Even sex can be an inherently playful act. All playfulness involves play, though play is not always playful. For example, an NFL quarterback losing a big game will still be *playing* football, but likely with grim determination rather than playfulness. When I do speak of *play*, it will be in reference to undertaking activities of any kind with a spirit of playfulness, rather than engaging in specific *play activities*.

Playfulness is essential to human flourishing. Abraham Maslow recognized it in his hierarchy of needs, situating it just under physical needs—food, water, shelter—and safety.[5] Play helps meet the deep human need for love and belonging, for esteem and self-actualization (the pursuit of growth, transformation, and wholeness). It is the oil that helps the engine of life run more smoothly. It's the glue that holds people—and cultures—together. It brings a lightness to the otherwise often heavy tasks of living.

One of best definitions I encountered was from Registered Play Therapist Malaika Clelland, who told me what play *does*, rather than what it *is*: "Play is anything that brings us joy and connection," she said. Bingo. Playfulness lights up the pleasurable areas of our brains, increasing levels of serotonin, dopamine, and a host of other happy chemicals. It deepens our bonds with one another, increasing trust and rapport. It opens our eyes to new possibilities and ways of thinking, helping us discover new ideas, perspectives, and solutions. When I asked Clelland how play helped in her counseling practice, she smiled and said, "It doesn't just *help*. The play is the therapy."[6]

Some of the best, most successful work is underscored by playfulness. Why else would billion-dollar companies like Google, Facebook, and Amazon feature corporate offices with ping-pong tables, creative seating, botanical gardens, and game rooms?[7] Apple's headquarters include a thousand bicycles for its employees to get around its vast campus. Sure, a shuttle might be more efficient, but would it be more *fun*?

Playfulness also helps us innovate. According to *Free to Learn* author Peter Gray, play "underlies many of the greatest accomplishments of adults."[8] Working hard, without breaks, whimsy, or creative reset time, can be the enemy of working *well*. Before Sal Khan founded Khan Academy, a brilliant—

and free!—online educational program, he was a hedge fund manager.

"I gotta stay here and look for more investment ideas!" he told his boss as his work day neared its end. His boss told him to go home. "Okay!" said Khan. "I'll go home and look for more investment ideas!" Finally, his boss clarified his expectations:

> You're not going to help anybody by just... having the appearance of motion. [If you tire] yourself out then you're just going to make bad decisions... When you're at work, have your game face on... but in order to do that, you're going to have to have other things in your life. You should read interesting books; you should recharge. That recharging is going to... keep you creative.[9]

This reframing not only transformed Khan's experience as a financial manager, it sowed the seeds of innovation that later helped him create a brilliant and equitable educational resource. Play can, quite literally, change the world.

While a playful spirit can help our minds flex into new ways of thinking, it also helps shield us from the fear of failure that can cripple true innovation. Playful people trust that mistakes have lessons to teach and missteps can turn into surprising wins. After all, everything from super glue to penicillin was created by accident: inventors noticed something new and interesting while in pursuit of designing something totally different. (Though, can we just pause for a moment and imagine how badly things may have gone for the person who accidentally invented super glue? Hoo boy.)

Creative thinkers are often masters of play. Albert Einstein described himself as untalented but "passionately curious."[10] Thomas Edison loved reading and reciting poetry. Martin Luther King Jr. sang in his church choir. Marie Curie kept a sample of radium on her bedside table as a nightlight. (Can't say I recommend that one.)

When we begin reembracing playfulness, approaching our work, rest, worship, and recreation with whimsy, incredible transformation is possible. We become less bound by the fear of failure and more open to transformation and ingenuity. We solve problems faster and with greater ease. We sleep better and experience less stress. We connect more easily with others and more readily see ourselves as part of a team. Most importantly, we are happier.

I'm not saying playfulness can cure clinical depression or bring world peace. Don't resign from the board of the Save the World Club just yet. But I am convinced that playfulness is quite a fantastic tool for helping us live out of the grayed-down doldrums and into the world of living color God created for us. It saved our little family's good humor—and probably our actual sanity as well—when we ended up stuck inside for months, pastoring and parenting through a public health crisis. Playfulness is a gift we're hardwired to love and flourish in, and it's flowing all around us, just waiting for us to step into its joyful stream.

It Begins

So if playfulness is really the answer—or at the very least, *an* answer—in our pursuit of happiness, *how* do we embrace it? Just trying to have more fun is rarely successful for long. In seasons of grief or exhaustion, when we're under unrelenting pressure or facing health challenges, the instruction to just be happier can feel oppressive at best, and downright cruel at worst. My friend Kay reminded me of a truly horrific line from *Fiddler on the Roof*: "God would like us to be joyful even when our hearts lie panting on the floor." Ugh, no. Truly, he would not. Last I checked, Jesus is screaming psalms about God's abandonment while in agony on the cross, not pre-quoting Paul's admonition to "Rejoice always!" while whistling a happy tune.

> OFTEN IT IS SUFFERING THAT BREAKS OUR HEARTS OPEN TO THE HUMAN NECESSITY OF PLAY.

Paradoxically, feelings of sadness, loss, longing, and even pain can—and often *do*—coexist with playfulness. Poet Ross Gay writes that "joy is the mostly invisible... underground union between us... We might call it sorrow..."[11] Playfulness doesn't stuff emotions down or ignore them; it doesn't will them away or tell them they're unwelcome. It notices, nurtures, and grants permission. Think of an Irish wake where tears mingle with stories of the beloved. Picture a dose of laughing gas taking the edge off a painful birth. Remember Jesus on the cross, reaching for the intrinsically poetic language of the psalmist to express his anguish.

Often it is suffering that breaks our hearts open to the human necessity of play. People who have it all together—or appear to—love to take themselves much too seriously. But those who know of their desperate need for God and their own fallibility and foibles can begin giving in to the release of playfulness. What grace! What relief! It is perhaps for this reason that Jesus speaks so strongly of the place of sinners in the kingdom of God and the struggle the self-righteous will have in entering it.

As Jesus puts it in Matthew's Gospel: "It is not the healthy who need a doctor, but the sick."[12]

If you lean more toward serious than joyful today, have no fear. Playfulness is a journey. Entrenched habits of unhealthy and unhelpful seriousness, like any longstanding habits, take more than just personal effort to overcome; ask anyone who's purchased a new piece of exercise equipment only to have it used as a laundry drying rack after only a few weeks on the job. (Not that, ahem, our rowing machine would ever be used for that purpose. We prefer to use it as a piece of modern art.)

In *Almost Holy Mama*, I wrote about how spiritual practices are so very good and life-giving in part because they work on us rather than forcing us to work hard at them. In my pursuit of happiness, I began to wonder if, in a similar vein, there might be a way to have playfulness work on me, since I certainly needed a lot of work. Playfulness that is lost does not easily return, and regular joy had evaporated from my life, dried up by drudgery, duty, and just getting through the day.

And here is what I love about the Gospel: wherever there's pain and difficulty, ache and sadness, grief and fear, and just getting through the day, there is also hope. This hope tends to show up when we least expect it, shining through the gloom, illuminating the darkness, flitting about like a lightning bug. Happiness, I was about to learn, doesn't have to be earned. If we are looking for playfulness and open to its magic, it will start to break in everywhere, performing its fantastic work on us and in us and through us. God is so good that way.

But we need to accept the invitation.

And therein lies the good news, and the tale of this book.

2

Why So Serious?

I take myself too seriously,
probably because I'm a human being.
—MAEVE HIGGINS

"How'd your doctor's appointment go?" my husband Daryl asked as he loaded the dishwasher.

"Oh, fine," I said. "He's sending me to an audiologist for tests since the ringing in my ear might signal hearing loss." I passed him a handful of spoons from the sink.

"Any idea what's causing it?"

"Probably a virus. Or an autoimmune reaction. Or maybe—ha ha—a brain tumor."

"Ha ha," he said. We both fell silent.

With three kids and three jobs between us, Daryl and I don't go to the doctor unless we discover a really weird mole or break a bone. So when my right ear started ringing—a loud, unyielding, high A-flat—I ignored it. It didn't hurt. Plus, our two oldest were late for swim lessons.

But when my nearly deaf grandmother and I went out for lunch and she asked why I kept yelling—I couldn't hear her over the din of the restaurant—I figured it was time for a checkup.

An audiologist confirmed my hearing loss and sent me back to the original doc, who ran again through the list of possible causes. The autoimmune reaction was rare.

"It could be a virus," he said. "But you haven't been sick. At this point—"

"I'm thirty-six years old," I protested. "Are you really saying I might have a—" my voice dropped to a whisper "—brain tumor?"

He waited a beat. Looked me straight in the eye.

"Premature," he said at last. "We need more tests."

Daryl and I serve together as pastors at a Presbyterian church. We talk a lot about the grace God gives when we finally accept that we don't control our lives. The beauty we discover as we learn to sit with uncertainty and embrace almost indescribable things like trust and hope.

Yet God-as-mystery can feel cruel. In the Bible, outside of Jesus—God made human—God tends to show up veiled, hidden, shrouded. God appears in a burning bush, a cloud, a whisper. Frequently God sends messengers rather than going personally—angels, prophets, and in one particularly bizarre case, a donkey.

Most often, God says nothing. God waits; we wait. The psalmist rails against this cosmic pause, writing: "How long, Lord? Will you forget me forever?"[13] How can we trust one who is so often inscrutable? So often silent?

After thirty years of practicing the faith I was preaching, perhaps I should have been more comfortable living in the mist. Daryl and I were no strangers to waiting: from the small infinity between when I was ready to get engaged and when he proposed, to the achingly long weeks of nauseous pregnancy, to the seemingly eternally sleepless Kingdom of Newbornlandia. For half a decade, Daryl inched closer to finishing a PhD. For months, we waited for the church we'd fallen in love with to offer us an interview to be their pastors. For an entire decade, I pitched the same book proposal to publishers, a proposal which never made it past the opening salvo. (Sometimes waiting *is* just folly.)

Still, as we waited together for a definitive diagnosis, mundane mishaps started to appear like symptoms of my impending doom. When I tripped on a Lego or forgot a parishioner's name or erupted in a shout because one of the kids splattered spaghetti sauce for the third time in a single meal, an icy vise of fear gripped my chest. It didn't help that the effects of kid-induced sleep deprivation and those of a brain tumor look essentially the same.

"It's going to be fine," Daryl told me as I lay in bed, staring at the ceiling. A leak in our air conditioner or a scratch on our car send him spiraling into panic and despair, but when the big, scary things of life hit, he is solid and unafraid. His faith wavers in the small stuff; mine falters in the big.

"Easy for you to say," I said. "If it *is* a tumor, complications include facial paralysis, deafness, balance issues, personality changes, and memory loss. On the other side of this, you'll still be you. I don't know who I will be."

He rolled over and took my hand, his beard wiry-soft against my cheek.

"Don't live there yet," he said.

As the days ticked toward my upcoming MRI—the test that would reveal God-in-the-cloud, giving us the answers we sought and maybe also the one we feared—our six-year-old needed to renew his library books. Our three-year-old built forts with every single pillow in the house. Our baby cooed and smiled and rubbed applesauce in her hair until tufts stuck out like feathers.

We held our worry close, not yet ready to receive the well-intentioned anxieties of family and friends and congregants. The life of our church—worship services and funerals, Holy

Yoga and AA meetings, English classes and Spanish classes and Sunday school—went on. We preached. Parented. Persevered.

For weeks, I snuck away from my office midday to pray in a nearby Catholic church where no one knew me or that I was a pastor. Its bubbling fountain masked the A-flat; its flickering candles reminded me that I was not alone in my prayers; and its giant crucifix just beyond the altar showed me a God who wasn't just silence and mystery, but blood and bone. I asked for healing and prayed for courage, but mostly I just sat there, quietly bewildered. Waiting.

"Take a nap," Daryl would say on Saturdays, gently nudging me toward our bedroom. If I hesitated, not wanting to give in to my deepest fear, he'd add, "It doesn't matter why you're tired."

In marriage, we pledged to love each other in sickness and in health, but what if this sickness would alter me until I was unrecognizable? How many blocks could be pulled from my tower of self until our marriage would crumble, Jenga-style? Unconditional acceptance is a beautiful sentiment, but I fell in love with a very specific person. I didn't walk down the aisle to Daryl just because he was tall, or because of the tender way he held my face between his hands the first time he kissed me, or because of his passion for ideas and Jesus and good guacamole and well-polished shoes. But in another very real sense, I *did*.

My singing voice first turned his head when we met as eighteen-year-olds in our college chapel. He asked me out on our first date because of our nerdy banter about literature, the crossword puzzles sticking out of my backpack, my abject failure at nearly all things math. Each quality that drew him to me was now in jeopardy from the tumor I was now almost certain I had.

Except being bad at math. I'd probably get to keep that.

I faced a terrifying question I'd never considered before: if my life was about to change irreversibly, what regrets did I have about how I'd been living up until this point? Our family life was loving and stable, but I couldn't shake the feeling that something was missing: an absence of an essential, biblical thing that would differentiate the mundane from the profoundly holy. We were missing *delight*. I'd been so busy working toward academic degrees and having babies and nurturing a church and chasing book dreams that somewhere along the way, I'd lost joy. I'd been trying so hard to serve God, I'd stopped just being with him, soaking in his love for me. I'd been working so diligently at maintaining a household and a marriage that I'd stopped being truly present to either. The proverbial trains were all running on schedule, but they were all headed to work.

I began to ponder. Whether or not I had a tumor, how could I find my way back to the country of delight?

In mid-summer, Daryl and I planned our family calendar for the year as always, talking through conferences we wanted to attend, church events, a late autumn trip into the mountains to take the kids to see snow. The scheduling felt foolish—and hopeful.

We celebrated Daryl's thirty-seventh birthday with dinner at In n' Out Burger and ice cream cake. The following Sunday, the few friends we'd told about my health found us after worship, looking at me with puppy dog eyes and asking, "But when will you *know*?"

"What?" I yelled over the worship band's postlude, leaning over to put my good ear closer to their mouths. "*What?*"

Days later, as I lay on the table, magnets clunking and whirring around my head, contrast-dye running into my veins, it hit me that I never would actually *know*. I might have a brain tumor; I might not. But the only certainty was that if Daryl and I lived long enough, there would be another day like this one for each of us, another season of chilling questions and foggy waiting. Life is uncertain. God is often hidden. But here's the thing: we are called toward joy anyway. Right now. Right here.

And joy, like all deep and beautiful and true things, is built on the intimate trust that God is who he says he is and will do what he says he will do, though storms will rage. Hope rests on the belief that, entwined with God and one another, we can somehow be strong enough to withstand winds that would fell us on our own, and say even in the midst of the howling gale, "It is well, it is well with my soul."

I didn't know how to begin saying this again. I'd said it as a child—not in so many words, but in an innate spirit of playfulness and trust, openness and delight. I witnessed this same spirit in my own children now, how effortlessly they'd celebrate, how quickly they'd move on from mistakes and scrapes, the ease with which they'd arrive at wonder, at awe, at connection. How could I rejoice again? I wasn't sure, but I knew one thing for certain: brain tumor or no brain tumor, I had to try.

A Communal Struggle

I wasn't the only one struggling to find happiness. Our culture has collectively swallowed the terrible myth that we must take almost everything—our lives, our work, our politics, our faith, our very selves—absolutely seriously. "My worry dolls are exhausted," joked comedian Aparna Nancherla.[14] Hers aren't alone. The majority of us are rowing the same boat of seriousness, together towing a humorless culture devoid of joy, unmoored from hope, and somber from stem to stern.

The statistics bear this out. Despite living in one of the wealthiest countries on earth, Americans are among the most anxious people on the planet. Notes Harvard Professor Arthur Brooks, "One of the greatest paradoxes in American life is that while, on average, existence has gotten more comfortable over time, happiness has fallen."[15] According to a Gallup study, "Americans were more likely to be stressed and worried than much of the world. [America] beat the global average by a full 20 percentage points. The U.S. even ties statistically with Greece, which has led the world on this measure every year since 2012."[16] You guys, we tied with Greece at long last! *Hip, hip, hoor*—oh, wait.

Brooks, a devout Catholic, connects our lack of happiness with our propensity for chasing the wrong things:

> Consumerocracy, bureaucracy, and technocracy promise us greater satisfaction, but don't deliver. Consumer purchases promise to make us more attractive and entertained; the government promises protection from life's vicissitudes; social media promises to keep us connected; but none of these provide the love and purpose that bring deep and enduring satisfaction to life... This is not an indictment of capitalism, government, or technology. They never satisfy—not because they are malevolent, but rather because they *cannot*.[17]

> It seems we seek happiness in all the wrong places and in all the wrong ways. The result is a culture devoid of joy, married to fruitless pursuits, and mired in hopelessness.

This relentless seriousness is wearing us all down to our frazzled cores. As Erin Griffith put it in the *New York Times*, "Welcome to hustle culture. It is obsessed with striving, relentlessly positive, devoid of humor, and — once you notice it — impossible to escape..."[18] The juxtaposition of relentless false positivity—EVERYTHING IS GREAT! THANKS FOR ASKING! WE ARE JUST GOOD, GOOD, GOOD OVER

HERE! HOW ARE YOU? ALSO GOOD? GREAT TO HEAR! HA HA!—and utter humorlessness—*We cannot joke about anything! Everything is too important!*—is truly fascinating. We've managed to paste on a cultural attitude of cheer, while quietly struggling to experience, embrace, or encounter any deep, lasting joy. A smiling seriousness has won the day.

Perhaps a definition may be helpful here. When I write of *seriousness*, I do not mean weightiness, earnestness, or thoughtfulness. Truth has weight to it. Earnestness can be defined as doing one's best out of genuine care and concern. Thoughtfulness is never not a good thing. Each of those is profoundly important, with shades of deep Christian virtue. But seriousness is a bird of a different feather. By seriousness, I mean a rigid, somber gravitas, a sense of over-responsibility, a desire to control, an unwillingness to experiment, and a profound fear of failure. Seriousness makes its bed with anxiety, anger, and frustration. It is a false grownupness that traps and binds us. It views even small matters as hills to die on. It is the opposite of wisdom, knowledge, and grace. It is utterly devoid of the whimsy, joy, and freedom of humor. It can also (obviously) make us pretty

> THE MAJORITY OF US ARE ROWING THE SAME BOAT OF SERIOUSNESS, TOGETHER TOWING A HUMORLESS CULTURE DEVOID OF JOY, UNMOORED FROM HOPE, AND SOMBER FROM STEM TO STERN.

cranky and unpleasant to be around. As a quote most often attributed to actress Eileen Brennan goes, "If we can't laugh at ourselves and the human condition, we're going to be mean."

The Trouble with Seriousness

Our society's epidemic of Serious-itis brings a host of devastating complications in its wake: everything from increasing interpersonal isolation (since, of course, vulnerability and seriousness do not mix) to unthinking legalism to a dearth of innovation and creativity. Small problems become devastating, failures feel fatal, and even innocent mistakes start to seem like fiery commentaries on our entire self-worth. Seriousness breeds fear and worry. It drains joy and shuts down learning and growth, in part because learning and growth both require the freedom to experiment—the chance to see what works and what doesn't without fear of permanent repercussions.

We can see this play out in real time with teenagers. Play researcher Stuart Brown shares the story of California's Jet Propulsion Lab (JPL), home to some of the brightest scientific minds in the country. Near the turn of the century, as employees hired in the 1960s began to retire and were replaced with new hires, problem-solving became ... well, a *problem*. Brown notes,

> Unlike their elders, the young engineers couldn't spot the key flaw in one of the complex systems they were working on, toss the problem around, break it down,

pick it apart, tease out its critical elements, and rearrange them in ways that led to a solution... The people JPL brought aboard had earned the highest grades at the best schools, but academic excellence was obviously not the most important measure of the graduates' problem-solving skills.

After researching the issue further, they discovered that the older employees, those who were adept at solving problems, had grown up tinkering—exploring mechanical things with their hands. Brown continues, "From that point on, JPL made questions about applicants' youthful projects and play a standard part of job interviews."[19] Imagine going to an interview and being asked not just about your experience and your grades, but also whether you'd ever taken a clock apart, just for fun! Tinkering is an inherently playful act, and one in which serious teenagers, propelled into academic overdrive and extracurricular achievement, have little time to engage.

The problem shows up across the board with our youth, not just in the more scientifically minded. For example, a couple of years ago, our church did a mission study, reaching out to organizations in the community to see what their needs were and how we might love and serve them as Jesus would. At one flagship high school, when we asked the principal what the biggest problem facing his students was, he responded with these haunting words: "Every one of our students is anxious."

"You mean *almost* all of them?" we asked.

"No," he said. "*All* of them."

College and Career Specialist Ann Bergen spends her days reminding public high school students that because they are unique and uniquely gifted, they don't need to fear that the world will end if they don't get top grades or brilliant test scores. "You can just see the cloud and the weight they're carrying in," she said. She sees it as a primary part of her job to help change their perspective from "who can I beat" to "what do I love to do?"

"I really get excited when students start realizing... it's about being who they were created to be," said Bergen. This shift helps free the students from the harmful belief that their worth depends upon getting into a top-tier college. Students walk into Bergen's office prepared for a college-and-career conversation to feel "like torture." What they aren't expecting is Bergen's joyful attitude toward the process.

"Sure, it's going to be work," she admits, "but think about it! We get to dream about what your life can be! When do you get to do that? Let's be five years old again and dream about what you used to like to do and stop worrying about whether you're good enough."[20] The playful posture Bergen models helps reorient the students to their ultimate hopes and goals—not beating out their peers on standardized tests, but crafting a life that will express their gifts and engage their passions. I wish I could send her to every single high school in America and, if she had any energy left, the rest of the world.

Our teenagers are just a microcosm of the broader epidemic of seriousness. We are, by and large, a serious people. Sadly, this shows up even when we engage in leisure activities. We tend to passively receive rather than actively engage; we consume rather than enter in. Our adult play is largely observational rather than participatory, distant instead of intimate, detached rather than connected. In other words, when we *do* play, it's not very fun. Americans spend over half their leisure time watching television (nearly three hours per day).[21] Pre-Covid theme parks were bursting at the seams with crowds[22] and professional sports teams were enjoying record-breaking profits (The NBA saw nearly a billion dollars in revenue growth from 2017 to 2018 alone).[23] The average American spent over $3,000 on entertainment in 2018 (up nearly 10% from 2016),[24] yet stress continued to increase and happiness kept decreasing.[25] Clearly, even many of the ways we are seeking to enjoy ourselves aren't bringing us lasting joy.

A Church Without Play

Tragically, Christians all too often succumb to the myth that church should be the most humorless of all places and its congregants the most somber of all people. I wish I could say that pastors were immune to this unfortunate belief, but we have all too often modeled it with gusto. We tell our folks, whether implicitly or in so many words: Sit down. Keep still. Arrange your facial features into appropriate reverence. *Shhhhhhhh.* Above all, remember that *this is serious.*

Order itself isn't the problem; it's actually quite essential for any gatherings where people hope to listen and reflect and pray. My friend Anna planted an outdoor church in downtown Los Angeles where she worked to balance welcoming the community's residents—including unhoused guests, some of whom struggled with mental illness—on the one hand and orderly worship on the other.

Writes Anna, "Rarely—no, never—did worship go exactly as I had planned. People didn't sit quietly and attentively. Albert would wander in, wearing his grubby white T-shirt, his baggy blue sweatpants, and his big sunglasses covering his puffy eyes. Some days he would doze through the sermon, but most days he'd have something to add ...

'Just two things, just two things, pastor,' he'd say, and I would reply, 'Not now, Albert. Now is a time for listening.'"[26] Anna found wise, kind, and playful ways to lean on the structure of worship to care for both Albert and the rest of the congregation. There would be time for speaking—much of it, in fact—but this moment was one for quiet reflection.

While we may feel that we owe it to our churches and our Savior to *take things seriously*, in truth, when we create a humorless culture, everyone suffers. When organizations fail to embrace the creative practices of invitation, permission, and release, they develop increasingly destructive patterns. According to Edwin Friedman, "The relationship between anxiety and seriousness is so predictable that the absence of playfulness in any institution—including church—is almost always a clue" to its unhealth. [27] Faith leaders who encourage playfulness stoke spiritual growth, increase organizational health, and help to free God's people from the stuckness of seriousness.

Plus, on a practical level, a playful posture simply helps faith stick better. Ask any longtime churchgoer what stuck with them from Sunday worship and I'm willing to bet not a single one would mention three points from a sermon, but nearly everyone would have a story of a playful instance that stuck with them.

When I began my first pastoral tenure at a congregation in rural Wisconsin, I spent months gathering stories from the people who called the church home. I heard of hopes and fears, sadness and celebration, petty crimes and professional grudges. I also heard quite a lot about play.

Half a dozen parishioners told me of the Sunday a former pastor used a tortoise to illustrate a point and then allowed the ancient creature to roam the chancel.

"I don't remember what he preached about," one farmer told me, "but that tortoise was a big hit."

One woman felt nervous when her toddler bolted from her lap in the middle of another pastor's sermon.

"I could have died," she said. "The whole church got quiet all of a sudden, but Pastor Jim just smiled and held out his hand. She just stood there and held his hand for the rest of the sermon."

"Do you remember what he said?" I asked.

"No," she admitted. "But I do remember how he smiled at her, and that I wasn't embarrassed anymore."

The other seriousness trap common to congregations comes when we begin to seek passive amusement from our worship, rather than encounter with the living God. This consumerism feeds seriousness in its own right, as churchgoers begin to see themselves as *observers* of the kingdom—commenting on spiritual things from a safe distance—rather than *participants* in it. We simply can't have it both ways. The Gospel is not observational; it's personal, all-encompassing, totally immersive. As Jesus tells Nicodemus in John 3, "Unless a person submits to this original creation—the 'wind-hovering-over-the-water' creation, the invisible moving the visible, a baptism into a new life—it's not possible to enter God's kingdom."[28]

Nicodemus wants to dip a toe in the metaphorical water, but Jesus waves to him from the top of the thirty-foot platform dive. Nicodemus is afraid of heights and would much rather just watch, thank you. Yet Jesus is too wild and kind to leave Nicodemus—or us—shivering by the edge of the pool. He beckons us higher in order to call us in deeper. It may feel safe on the sidelines, but all the fun is to be had in the pool, and it's only when we let go, dive in, and submerge ourselves in the shimmering waters that we begin to learn that God will always keep us afloat.

Maybe if churches were a little bit more like high dives, we'd all be in a better place. What if, as the writer Aarik Danielsen so beautifully put it, "They knew we were Christians by our play?"[29]

Joining In

Knowing I wasn't alone in my struggles with seriousness, I sent out an SOS to a dozen friends asking what they did for fun and whether they'd be willing to invite me to join them, hoping that playing with them would help spark a playful change in me. It took a while to get answers back from most, both because they didn't think I actually meant it, and because I tend to befriend people who have *also* become boring-and-serious-adults. Like attracts like, and all that. Plus, to be honest, Super Fun People™ kind of terrify me.

IT MAY FEEL SAFE ON THE SIDELINES, BUT ALL THE FUN IS TO BE HAD IN THE POOL.

"What's *wrong* with them?" I asked my husband as we watched a video of my sister and brother-in-law doing the "polar bear plunge"—jumping through a hole chopped in the ice into the frigid waters of Minnesota's Lake Vermilion in January. I *may* have considered doing that for a million dollars. Possibly. But no one was paying Caitlyn and Jared. It wasn't even for charity. They were risking frostbite *purely for fun* alongside a dozen other people who had clearly also misplaced the good-decision-making parts of their brains.

Little by little, my friends' responses to my email trickled in. I was invited to go mountain biking, beach walking, line dancing, and boogie boarding. Folks sent me their favorite book recommendations and challenged me to bedazzle cement farm animals and leave them in my neighbors' yards. A couple of young adults took me to an archery range. Our babysitter told me to climb a tree.

When the responses started to slow, I took matters into my own hands, cornering my friend Kassy in the church parking lot and asking her to take me surfing.

"I'm afraid of sharks," I told her.

"No problem," she said.

"I'm not a *great* swimmer," I said.

"That's okay."

"I don't actually even want to go," I said.

"It's fine," she said. Kassy is built straight out of kindness. "Really. I will take you."

But mostly I received the same basic response from people over and over again: that by and large, my friends had forgotten how to play; that they weren't even sure what to make of the question. That they *used* to have fun, when they were kids or back in college, but then life became very life-y, draining both the time and the energy for playfulness.

My friend Chris responded,

> Do you mean "play as in play-with-your-kids"? I sometimes do that and enjoy it ... But if you mean "play" as in "have fun, as an adult, by yourself or with other adults ..." I am terrible at it. For years, I've wanted to get back into playing tennis or to learn mountain biking, but amid all the pressures of life these past few years, that has definitely felt like a luxury I cannot afford in terms of time or money. One of the unexpected costs of the PhD is that while many of my peers found hobbies and played in their early 30s, I hunkered down to work and lost those years and experiences.[30]

While most of us didn't spend our thirties earning a PhD, nearly all of my friends expressed a similar loss and longing. They *missed* having fun. They longed for the unencumbered state of whimsy, joy, and release. They'd also started to believe that having more fun would require significant amounts of time or money or both, a myth it would take me a while to dispel myself. Still, to a person, they thought—they *knew*—that playfulness would improve their lives and would make them happier; they just weren't sure how to reclaim it or where to find it. I wasn't, either.

The gradual but continual loss of play in adulthood is a real problem. Increased somberness takes a toll. Too much seriousness is linked to hopelessness. It robs us of joy and fills us with dread; it causes us to remain stunted when we are designed for growth. And not only that—Brown puts the risk in stark terms: "If we stop playing, we share the fate of all animals that grow out of play. Our behavior becomes fixed. We are not interested in new and different things. We find fewer opportunities to take pleasure in the world around us."[31] I'd discovered this to be true, not just for me but for American culture at large, in both the statistical and the experiential analyses. Seriousness was beginning to win the day, and we were all suffering.

Still, I reflected upon the fact that I wasn't doing anything *wrong*— not really—spending my days serving my church, nurturing my marriage, tending to my children, trying to exercise and eat well and roll the trash cans in from the curb on time. But even with my earnest desire to faithfully follow Jesus in every area of my life, my happiness had largely vanished, replaced instead with a task-oriented drudgery, producing a series of utilitarian, gray days blending into one another without a spark of color.

> WE ARE NOT GIVEN THE GIFT OF LIFE TO SPEND IT BY SIMPLY AVOIDING THE BAD. WE ARE CALLED TO EMBRACE AND SEEK AFTER THE GOOD WITH ALL THAT WE ARE.

So what gives?

Well, here's the thing: there is a distinct and important difference between simply not doing anything *wrong* and living into the fullness of life that God sets before us. When God sets Adam and Eve in the garden amidst gorgeous flora and peaceful fauna, he proclaims it good. When God sings over the lovers in Song of Songs, he invites them to drink deeply. When Jesus speaks to his weary followers, he begs them to come to him, the master whose burden is light. We are not given the gift of life to spend it by simply avoiding the bad. We are called to embrace and seek after the good with all that we are. This is our one pass through this earthly veil, and we might ask what we will do with these priceless, fleeting, finite days. Our answer must not be: "The dishes. Mostly the dishes. And usually with a chip on my shoulder."

But then, what *must* our answer be?

I had many more questions than answers. Questions like: how do we jettison this soul-sick seriousness and rediscover God's gift of joy? Is it even possible? Is adulthood simply enduring until we die? Or is there something better—something more?

I was beginning to suspect that there was.

And that it was even better than I had hoped.

3

Jazzy Jesus

*The Son of Man came feasting
and you called him a lush.*

—LUKE 7:34 MSG

The doctor had been shooting the breeze with me for five minutes before I finally pressed him for the news.

"Oh!" he exclaimed. "I almost forgot. Your scans came back perfectly. You don't have a tumor!" Relief mixed with anger washed over me—why had he left me in agony waiting for the results? How about a *phone call*, sir?

I called Daryl after the appointment, crying tears of reprieve. We wouldn't have to Google "best brain surgeons" or figure out our financial liability for a procedure and recovery that'd cost hundreds of thousands of dollars. I wouldn't need to learn how to walk and talk again. Life could go on as normal—or as normal as it could be with my one good ear. This was wonderful.

Yet as the news sunk in, I couldn't shake the completely bizarre feeling that it was also a tiny little bit *not* wonderful. I'd just learned I didn't have a brain tumor—after a month of increasing certainty that I did. I should be walking on air, but I wasn't. Instead of pure relief, I felt tinged with sadness, melancholy, regret, despair. Of course, the cause of my hearing loss was still unexplained, and that uncertainty was an uncomfortable emotion to bear. Yet those hours stolen in the stained-glass parishes nearby had driven me to my knees with a singular purpose: asking God to spare me from a brain tumor. God had. So why was I struggling to embrace this hoped-for reality?

"I don't think I actually know how to be happy," I told Daryl later that night, lying in the middle of our bed, staring at the ceiling while he folded a basket of laundry. "I was so ready to accept the worst that I don't know how to rejoice in the best."

Brené Brown calls our propensity to prepare for the worst "dress-rehearsing for tragedy" and notes that we are especially prone to it "in moments of deep joy." Though I'd gotten the news I'd hoped for, I was already well primed for disaster, making me unsure how to truly take in this good news. Pain and fear felt safer than celebration. Brown calls joy the most vulnerable emotion, and that rang true for me.[32] Something needed to change. I needed to learn how to live in the country of happiness once again, making peace with the vulnerability it required. I didn't want to live the rest of my life holding happiness at bay.

Still, I wasn't sure where to start. Daryl and I had both been running full-tilt for over a decade. Much of our marital life had been dedicated to the single-minded pursuit of various achievements: degrees, vocations, pastoral calls, publishing goals. We were no strangers to hustle culture. Now, without such a full-court press—he'd finally finished his PhD; I'd written my book—we felt unmoored and a little lost. We had little reason to be unhappy, but we simply were. Though no part of me *wanted* a brain tumor, at least a sliver of me knew it would have given me a clear purpose once again—something to fight against. I was a pretty good fighter.

"Well," Daryl asked, "when do you feel the happiest?"

"I have no idea," I said. "I don't really *do* happy. I mean, who has time? I just need some sort of plan. Or maybe a class. Ten days to a happier Courtney."

He chuckled. "I don't think that's going to work." He paused, dropping a pile of folded shirts at the foot of the bed. "I also think it's going to take you a bit longer than ten days to get to the bottom of your seriousness."

He was right. But then ... *how?*

Driving home from work the next day, I flipped on the radio. Someone—probably the three-year-old who liked to "drive" the car while it was parked in front of our house—had changed all my presets. I was expecting NPR, and instead the car flooded with jazz. I laughed.

And suddenly I knew where to begin.

Nearly a decade ago, a couple of years into my first pastorate, I took a two-day spiritual retreat in a nearby city. Since we weren't close to any retreat centers, I booked a room at a hotel, filled the mini-fridge with snacks, stacked my Bible and journal on the bedside table, and entered into a haven of two days with nothing on my plate but Jesus and rest. It seemed idyllic. Peaceful. Perfect. Which is probably why I found myself face down on the carpet within an hour, crying my eyes out.

I can't do this, Jesus, I prayed. *This pastoring thing is too hard. I don't know if I'm even built for it. Nothing is as I thought it would be. I can't figure it out, and I'm so, so tired.*

The knowledge from seminary and the adrenaline of a first call only carry a new pastor so far. Two years in, I was running on fumes. My plan for saving the world by just trying hard and working every possible minute was obviously a failed one. Worse yet, somewhere along the way I'd bought into the myth that to be deep and meaningful and *true*, people and practices must be grave. I'd begun to act pastorally somber, and this new, heavy, rigid persona was clashing with my deep, God-given desires for joy, flexibility, and creativity. I'd descended into a profound seriousness, and both my ministry and my soul had begun to suffer.

I was exhausted, and there were no glimmers of happiness on the horizon. Just a frozen winter blending into a frozen spring, Daryl chipping away at his PhD, me sitting through another meeting, preaching another sermon, and visiting another hospital room while wearing sensible shoes and praying for summer to come. I was starving for light and color and *fun*, but how could I paint if I'd given away all of my metaphorical brushes?

As I cried and prayed in that hotel room overlooking a Chicago freeway, I felt God impress a simple instruction on my heart:

You're going to need to learn to play jazz.

I laughed aloud, my tears of desperation turning to tears of laughter, the pile of Kleenex at my side growing ever taller. Here's the thing: I *hate* jazz. I took one semester of jazz piano in college and quit because it didn't make a lick of sense to me (pun intended). I love rhythm and meter, rules and regulations, do's and don'ts, clarity and structure, and when my instructor told me to play a couple of riffs off the top of my head, just for fun, improv-style, I promptly walked to the registrar and asked to drop the class.

I don't even like *listening* to jazz, unless I'm driving fast late at night and pretending I'm in *Ocean's 11*. But here was God, seemingly saying to me, "You're trying to muscle your way through things. Stop it. Learn to improvise. Have a little fun. *It will work better.*"

I spent the rest of my retreat searching the Scriptures for Jazzy Jesus, and it turned out he was all over my Bible: spitting in the mud to heal a blind man; pushing his way through a bellicose crowd; using whatever was near him—fields, sheep, seeds, birds—to illustrate his points; answering a question sideways rather than straight on. Master of improv, Jesus.

GOD IS IN THE BUSINESS OF UP-ENDING THE STATUS QUO, THROWING OUT CURVEBALLS, SURPRISING US ALL.

Back at my church office later that week, I printed out an illustration of a jazz trumpeter and taped it to the wall, a visual reminder of a playful God. It didn't cure all that ailed me, but it was a pivotal beginning. Turns out even jazz has its place in the kingdom, both because it teaches us to live playfully and because, as the jazz great Wynton Marsalis once said, "Jazz teaches you about yourself."[33]

The same improvisational rhythms that give jazz its distinctiveness show up in abundance in the economy of God. Divine evidences of playful hope are everywhere. God is in the business of upending the status quo, throwing out curveballs, surprising us all.

"Oh," Jesus says, "you thought the kingdom of heaven would come with military might? Guess again! It's like a mustard seed, a pearl. It's like yeast that's been worked all through the dough."

In her poem "Luke 14: A Commentary," Kathleen Norris describes Jesus saying such absurd things his disciples can't help but laugh. Invite the poor to the banquet? There will always be enough room? Hilarious. She continues:

> Charlie
> Chaplin put it this way: "I want to play
> the role of Jesus. I look the part.
> I'm a Jew.
> And I'm a comedian."[34]

Following Jesus is an inherently creative act. There are principles—discipleship, obedience, service—but *how* to implement them is left up to us, with wisdom and guidance from the church. Those popular *What Would Jesus Do?* bracelets from the 1990s were a silly but often helpful reminder of what it would mean for the divine Savior to walk around in our shoes, in our context. I remember a guy in my high school band sporting a red one as he marched alongside me in the 4th of July parade.

"Hmm," I wondered, "how *would* Jesus play the trombone?" With joy and panache, no doubt, and all his heart.

Of course, God calls us to work for the good of the kingdom and the salvation of the world. To grieve with those who grieve. To lament and pray and fast. To feel the weight of our sin and repent of it. To take public health directives to heart, even when they're inconvenient. We ignore the needs of humanity at our own peril—and theirs. But even with all the pain and poverty, violence and vitriol, war and weariness, God never calls us to deadly seriousness. To earnestness, yes. To faith and good works, absolutely. But not to white-knuckled, try-harder humorlessness. Never to a descent into seriousness at the expense of joy and connection.

The thread of playfulness is woven throughout Scripture. The Psalms fairly ring with whimsy. (Don't get me wrong—they ring with plenty else, too: anguish and rage and lament—but happiness is there in spades.) David dances in such a frenzy before God that onlookers think he has imbibed too much wine. The same is true at the outpouring of languages at Pentecost in the book of Acts where the crowds, baffled as to what to make of the raucous outpouring of communication, find themselves at last understanding and understood.

It's easy to sanitize this awe, however. Too often we read over passages too quickly or too somberly, sitting stiffly in our pews and turning the vibrant colors of life and light, poetry and image to dusty grays, stripping biblical wonder of its joyfulness. We disconnect it from the messy stories of Scripture where those who experienced the Lord were never the same again. This type of playfulness—wild, free, abandoned to the love and mercy of God—well, it

FOLLOWING JESUS IS AN INHERENTLY CREATIVE ACT.

might not seem quite *proper*. Isn't it Jesus who asks us to do things decently and in order? Oh wait, that is my own stuffy denominational guidelines. Never do we find Jesus asking us to embrace greater rigidity for the kingdom. Instead, he grants us permission to live in improvisational freedom. To step into the divine joy born of good news, glad tidings, and abundant life. To *playfulness*—the very, very fullest, best, most freeing kind of gift.

Jesus knew how to riff.

I was just beginning to learn.

PART II

The 10 Invitations of Playfulness

The beginning is always today.
—MARY WOLLSTONECRAFT

My youngest sister Caroline was a handful as a child, with boundless energy and strong opinions. When my parents got tired of her shrieks of displeasure over such terrible things as having to *put her shoes on* or *eat her dinner*, they'd send her to sit on a bench in our entryway, which we affectionately referred to as "The Happy Chair." This worked well for a time; they'd slide the pocket door nearly shut and tell her, gently but firmly, "You can have a tantrum, but we don't have to watch." We passed a good number of meals this way, my middle sister and me smirking at each other across the table, grateful for a moment of near-peace from Caroline's antics.

Caroline would rage and seethe for a bit, and then her little fingers would appear on the side of the pocket door that separated entryway from kitchen, sliding it open, her tear-streaked face screwed into a grimacing attempt at a smile.

"I happy now," she'd say.

"Welcome back," my parents would respond.

The Happy Chair lasted a successful few months until one day my dad noticed that the kvetching had stopped, but Caroline still hadn't reappeared. He slid the door open to reveal a chipmunk-cheeked four-year-old with a line of sugary drool sliding down the corner of her mouth.

"What in the world...?" he began, before noticing the candy, gum, and cough drop wrappers strewn about the floor.

"Barb!" he said, "Caroline went through our coat pockets!"

Thus ended the Happy Chair.

I'll be honest—I used to approach my own happiness much like the Happy Chair, believing that if I just *tried hard enough* to drag myself into a more joyful state of being, I could do it. While this isn't totally untrue—feelings are educable, after all, and sometimes acting how we *want* to feel can help us get there—it's usually not the smoothest path. It is certainly not the easiest. Happiness can be learned, but it can't be forced (naughty, tantrum-throwing four-year-olds notwithstanding.) Happiness can be welcomed, but it can't be manufactured. Much of our task is simply to receive it with open hands when it knocks on our door.

And that, friends, is delightfully good news. We may not be able to will ourselves into better moods, but we can choose to say yes to the invitations of playfulness. When we give ourselves permission to play, the release of playfulness does the rest. The same pattern appears time and time again: invitation, permission, release.

The more I studied and experimented, the more I noticed the same ten invitations of playfulness rising to the surface. (And remember, they're *invitations*, not commandments! These are supposed to be fun!) Each was applicable in almost every season of life and adaptable to children and seniors, rural and urban dwellers, parents and grandparents, marrieds and singles, men and women alike. As is true with all echoes of Gospel

> WE MAY NOT BE ABLE TO WILL OURSELVES INTO BETTER MOODS, BUT WE CAN CHOOSE TO SAY YES TO THE INVITATIONS OF PLAYFULNESS.

truth, time and place don't alter the underlying river of grace. Though their shapes may look a little different from season to season and age to age, the themes of playfulness translate well to whatever our circumstances may be.

The ten invitations of play are as follows:

1. Rest well
2. Be a kid again
3. Connect
4. Improvise
5. Do useless things
6. Seek adventure
7. Invest in community
8. Play small
9. Fail regularly
10. Take off your shoes

Each is incredibly powerful. When we say yes to them, giving ourselves permission to enter into their magical depths, they begin to lift us up and renew our spirits. The release of playfulness does all the work; our job is simply to say yes.

The rest of this book devotes a chapter to each invitation in turn. Read them in order or start with whichever one makes you smile. (After all, that's what it's all about!)

Here's to playfulness.

Here's to happiness.

Here's to you!

1

Rest Well

I lift my heart like a bowl
to catch the golden light
it fills to the brim,
then overflows

—STEPHANIE JENKINS, "DRINK IT IN"[35]

"Oh, did you want coffee?" Daryl smiled at me with Felicity on his hip. She'd woken up again at 4:45 am, a time of day that should never be witnessed by a human who isn't either in A) college or B) active labor. He'd graciously taken her out for a post-dawn stroll around the neighborhood, but I still hadn't been able to fall back to sleep. I stumbled into the kitchen at 5:30, freshly showered, completely exhausted, and totally grumpy.

I stared blankly at Daryl. He held up the empty coffee pot.

"Coffee," he said. "Did you want some?" I blinked and willed my mind to focus.

"Yes," I said through gritted teeth. "Of course I want coffee."

"I'm joking, Court," he said, shifting our little rooster of a child onto his other hip. "I'm brewing it right now."

"Oh," I collapsed into a kitchen chair. "I'm sorry. I just ... I am so tired." This wasn't the first morning that week we'd had a 4:45 am wake-up call. Nor would it be the last. We'd tried everything to put an end to these early risings, from giving Felicity an extra nap (was she overtired?) to taking away her nap entirely (perhaps she wasn't tired enough?) to feeding her a high-fat, high-protein snack right before tucking her in (maybe she was just hungry?). No dice. Just misery.

He poured the water into the coffee maker's reservoir and started the machine.

"I know," he said. "I'm tired, too."

"I know," I said. "I love you."

"I love you, too."

"I love you too, baby girl," I said to Felicity, tickling her pajama-toed foot. "But if you want parents who are any fun at all, *this has got to stop*."

As I began seeking out a more playful existence, I quickly stumbled across what keeps so many of us from play: life can be quite exhausting. Time feels short, loads weigh heavy, and the immediate and important quickly drown out the ideal and hoped-for. It can seem formidable—if not impossible—to pursue happiness when there are so many other essential tasks begging for attention. How are we supposed to embrace play when finances are tight, friendships are strained, and flu season (or worse!) is here? What about when our boss is impossible? When the rent increases, the refrigerator breaks, or the student loans come due? When—and I'm speaking hypothetically here—a toddler decides that sleep is for the weak? Not to mention the difficulties we face in the more desperate or devastating seasons of life when grief arrives, illness turns chronic, or all hope seems lost.

Whether we face disasters or simply the daily grind, when we are worn ragged we will struggle to play. My sharpest descent into seriousness happened during graduate school and the years immediately following, as we welcomed three babies in six years. My next bout with it came when schools shut down with barely a day's notice and I was suddenly responsible to homeschool a first grader and a preschooler, care for a toddler, and pastor a church through a global crisis. When our margins wear away and rest becomes elusive, naturally playfulness—and its close cousins, creativity, innovation, and fun—soon follow suit.

Indeed, rest is one of the greatest deficits we face in the modern West, and this contributes significantly to our unhealthy seriousness as a culture. More than a third of adults don't get enough sleep;[36] we fill the bulk of our free hours with television (which is not often deeply restful);[37] and we live glued to our smartphones, leaving little margin for our souls to breathe.[38] When the pandemic swept through, the usual out-of-house outlets many of us went to for recreation—the gym, the cooking club, the library story hour—took a huge hit, leaving us even more depleted and isolated. Exhaustion is no friend to happiness.

And herein lies the first invitation of playfulness: to play well, we must rest well. It is nearly impossible to accept the invitations of play if we are completely exhausted. Without our most basic needs—food, water, shelter, and sleep—being met, playfulness becomes a serious uphill battle. First, we rest.

Because God knew we would need this spiritual reset, a regular, repeated break from the labor of our lives, he gave us the gift (and command!) to remember the Sabbath day and keep it holy. By engaging in regular Sabbath rest, we slowly learn that joy begins in acquiescing to our limits and accepting the invitation to let God restore our souls. This is, in its own gentle way, a type of play. On the Sabbath, we give ourselves permission to rest in the loving embrace of the Savior who created and sustains us. We release ourselves to God, in whom our happiness exists.

PLAYFULNESS INVITES US TO CELEBRATE A WEEKLY SABBATH— A DAY SET APART FOR WORSHIPFUL, RESTORATIVE REST.

A Sabbath Challenge

Even when we admit how very much we need it, it is hard to accept the invitation to Sabbath. It is difficult to give ourselves permission to stop *doing*. It always has been. Notes Wayne Muller, "Our culture invariably supposes that action and accomplishment are better than rest, that doing something—*anything*—is better than doing nothing."[39] Wendell Berry describes these pressures in this way: "There is no such thing as enough. Our bellies and our wallets must become oceanic, and still they will not be full. Six workdays in a week are not enough. We need a seventh. We need an eighth ... Everybody is weary, and there is no rest ..."[40]

This unhealthy impulse rises up even more strongly in times of uncertainty, difficulty, and crisis. For example, in the middle weeks of March 2020, when my home state of California received stay at home orders and many employees transitioned to working remotely, the productivity of these employees actually *rose*. People faced a terrifying health crisis, the stress of trying to find food staples on empty store shelves, and the difficulty of schooling children at home—*and still the workday lengthened by an average of three hours.*[41] This is bananas, people. Utterly bananas. And yet, Daryl and I absolutely fell right into this trap, too. It was our children—well trained in the joys of the Sabbath—who reminded us that holy rest wasn't optional. Nothing like getting schooled by a four-year-old, especially when he's right.

Stress, trauma, and hardship easily fool us into thinking rest is a luxury, something we can finally get to when all the other work is done. Our default isn't to stop or recalibrate, even when we have desperate need to do so. Yet crisis work is endless. The work of life, even relatively normal, everyday life, is ongoing. And when we fail to set our labors aside for even a short time, we will find that *we* are not endless.

Old Testament scholar Walter Brueggemann makes the connection between our frantic lives of today and Pharaoh's Egypt where God's people were forced into slave labor. "Christians may find the Sabbath commandment the most urgent and the most difficult of all the commandments," he writes. We may not be enslaved by Pharaoh, but we've become slaves to our own doings and goings and strivings. This is why,

> LETTING GOD TAKE THE REINS FOR THE DAY IS A PROFOUNDLY PLAYFUL ACT.

as Brueggemann says, "the departure into restfulness is both urgent and difficult."[42] Regular, routine, repeated rest is not something we can put off until the children are grown or the workload abates or the crisis has ended. We need it *now*. But as Berry notes, there is no rest unless we "adopt the paradoxical and radical expedient of *just stopping*."[43]

And this is the true beauty of Sabbath rest—we don't have to work at it; instead, it will work *on us* if we simply cease our labors. Letting God take the reins for the day is a profoundly playful act. (Of course, God holds those reins every day; but in acquiescing to Sabbath, we remind ourselves in an even deeper way that God is ultimately in control.) As we stop and rest, we take our hands off the wheel and leave the steering to the one who can see the whole road ahead. In leaving emails unsent, laundry unfolded, and errands un-run, we begin to learn that God can be trusted, that we aren't what we do, and that our God-given limits are grace, not burden.

Our family's weekly Sabbath reminds me in a profound and fundamentally important way that I am not irreplaceable, and that the work of God and the church—even without me! who knew?—will always go on. What grace to be reminded of our place in the world—infinitely loved and of priceless value, and yet not the only cog in the grand mechanism of God's big, beautiful world or even our little churchy corner of it.

Much like our churches are sanctuaries in space—worshipful places to meet regularly with God—the Sabbath is a sanctuary in time. As Eugene Peterson notes, "Sabbath is the time set aside to do nothing so that we can receive everything."[44] It is nearly impossible to overstate its gift and importance. If we never put down our heavy yoke of toil, worry, and striving, we will always struggle to play.

Perhaps that's why God made the Sabbath an imperative—out of love, and knowing us a little too well. If a gentle invitation and a divine nudge won't do, perhaps putting it in a list of commandments will. If permission isn't enough, maybe requirement will be.

After all, what do you have to lose but your ragged edges?

A Sabbath Delight

The Sabbath holds vital space for my husband and me and our children to play. Without it, I shudder to think how much more serious we might become! When our oldest son started kindergarten, we began practicing our family Sabbath from Friday afternoon—when we picked him up from school—to Saturday at the same time. (Sundays are commonly a workday for those of us in ministry. I know, right? How *rude*.) We set aside twenty-four hours for "praying and playing," as Eugene Peterson puts it,[45] logging off our email, putting away our to-do lists, and winding down to a near-stop. No one is in a hurry. That alone marks it as a day of celebration and rest.

Watching our kids' joy during this regular, unstructured time of tinkering and puttering and resting play, their deep contentment in the slowness of the Sabbath rhythm, and the way they look forward to a regular, holy day when their parents are not on the run, is a continual lesson for us. On Sabbath we sit on the living room floor. We drink warm coffee instead of cups that have grown cold due to the hurry and distraction of the day. We say yes to the Legos, the puzzles, the blanket fort, the chess match. Or we say no to parental-activity-provisions and let the children explore solitary pursuits or games with one another while we read things that interest us (and, for once, don't involve construction equipment, chocolate factories, or patting a bunny).

While the *togetherness* of Sabbath is one of its gifts, the solitariness of Sabbath is lovely as well. Here we find the uniqueness of Sabbath speaking to our individual circumstances. If you live alone, you may choose to spend Sabbath with a dear friend or family member, to drink deeply of the love of a community of grace. If you care for an aging relative or young children, you may need a Sabbath break from the constant grind of caregiving and revel in a few hours alone.

On our family Sabbath, Daryl and I work to give each other blocks of time completely to ourselves—relief we often crave and cherish the most in these days of the relentless physical exhaustion of parenting tiny kids. By Sabbath, what I usually want most in the world is an hour or two to simply think my thoughts

AN UNHURRIED LIFE INVITES JOY. A SOUL AT REST IS OPEN TO BLESSING.

without someone hanging on me begging for a snack. I return from my time away—even if "away" is simply the recliner in the bedroom behind a closed door—made new, or, at the very least, with my patience reserves a little less depleted.

As we continue cultivating the practice of Sabbath, playfulness bubbles up more easily as well. An unhurried life invites joy. A soul at rest is open to blessing. Engaging in Sabbath practices regularly resets our schedules and our priorities, helping us to reorder the rest of our days in light of God's love for us and his call on our lives.

As we begin to taste this goodness, we will inevitably look forward to it more and more. Ruth Haley Barton writes of the shift that begins to happen: "The truth is, sabbath keeping is a discipline that will mess with you, because once you move beyond just thinking about it and actually begin to practice it, the goodness of it will capture you, body, soul and spirit. You will long to wake up to a day that stretches out in front of you with nothing in it but rest and delight."[46] Awakening these deep, God-given longings is part of stepping into the waters of playfulness. Numb people don't play well. Sabbath practices put us back in touch with our nerve-endings once again.

Resting well, as God intended us to do, restores our souls, reawakens our imaginations, and reorients us to God as the source of our joy and gladness. We are simply not created to keep going forever—or even for a week!—without the rest God commands.

Plus, it doesn't hurt that—at least in our household—we begin the Sabbath with donuts.

The Mechanics of Sabbath

It can seem tricky to translate an ancient communal practice into one that makes sense today, particularly when even our churches don't tend to encourage honoring the Sabbath in any significant way. It seems to be taken almost universally as the most optional of the Ten Commandments. The good news is that accepting God's invitation is fairly simple. It begins with just three basic steps.

First, we must prepare. It will take intention to cease our work for one day each week. Prepare your calendar and keep it clear. Work obligations and the addendums to everyday life (Birthday parties! Doctor's visits! Just one... quick... meeting!) will crowd out the Sabbath if we don't guard the day. This isn't to say there won't be exceptions—I wrote much of this chapter on the drive up to our high school youth group ski trip on my Sabbath—but those should be rare. In these special cases, another day should be substituted as the Sabbath within the same week, if at all possible. We always need the spiritual and mental reset, even if our calendar ends up topsy-turvy from time to time.

While the Jewish Sabbath was practiced from sundown Friday to sundown Saturday, most Christians choose to take Sunday as their Sabbath so regular church worship can be part of the day. If you are employed at a church or a business that requires Sunday work, you will likely need to find another day for Sabbath rest. The day you choose is less important than the regularity of it; whenever possible, the Sabbath should fall at the same time each week, both so you don't have to worry about scheduling it *and* so that it repeats itself every seven days. If you cannot devote a whole day to Sabbathing, set aside at least a half-day, or even a few hours.

As part of our preparation, Daryl and I like to tidy the house a bit before our Sabbath arrives, so we can really feel at ease within our four walls. Some people rest well with mountains of laundry around, but I'm not one of them. I keep a line in my work email signature to let people know that messages I receive on that day will be read and responded to on the following day. You may want to cook a meal or two in advance. A family friend of ours doesn't cook on her Sabbath, since she prepares the majority of their meals the other six days. Getting ready is key: as Abraham Heschel's beautiful book, *The Sabbath*, notes, "Preparation for a holy day ... is as important as the day itself."[47]

Secondly: welcome the Sabbath by stopping your work, engaging in worship, and enjoying rest. We are free to do anything that isn't work-related, but what we do is less important than the act of stopping regular labors to pause in worshipful rest. Listen to your body, your mind, and your soul—are you tired? Worried? Angry? Scared? Give yourself the luxury of attending to your soul before the Lord in worship and prayer.

On the Sabbath, give yourself over to practices that are truly worshipful and restful for you. Think of what types of play might be most restorative—tinkering? Canning peaches? Hiking? Be delightfully unproductive and do nothing at all.

Watch the angle of the sun change from your window as the hours wear on. Sit on the lawn, at the park, or in the snow. For the love of all that is good and holy, take a nap. Quiet, restful presence is its own act of worship.

If at all possible, put away your digital devices and turn off your screens; we don't relax during our downtime nearly as well when we are constantly connected or entertained away from our deeper rhythms. Closing the portal to the entire wider world in order to attend to our souls and those who are nearest us is one of the most restful things we can do.

On our family Sabbath, we eat together, play together, go off in pairs or singles to spend time with Jesus and our own thoughts, leave our phones plugged in on the kitchen counter instead of buzzing in our pockets, and we rest. During my solo time, I usually hit the exercise bike in the garage (my pent-up angst from the previous week needs to go somewhere, and exercise is a great way to alleviate it!) and then I nap and read. Daryl most often works on an outdoor project to help still his busy hands and mind. For those of you who have tiny children or are caregivers, I highly recommend this turn-taking. Because our children are incredibly early risers, they are allowed to greet the day with a parent-approved movie so Daryl and I can sleep in past five. (Sometimes digital devices can be grace, too!)

Finally, when the day is at its close, thank God for the Sabbath and prayerfully re-enter your week. By the end of our family

Sabbath, each person has begun to return to God anew, to return to ourselves, and to return to one another. We are different. More at peace. Happier. The gift of the Sabbath spills over into every other day, and at the day's end we find ourselves thankful for its gifts and looking forward to returning to its delights once again in a week's time.

The study and practice of the Sabbath have been making a quiet resurgence in recent years. I'm so glad to see it. Almost nothing is as central to our long-term spiritual, emotional, and ecclesial health as embracing worshipful rest. Indeed, the people of God are set apart—made holy—for this very thing. We are simply not designed to go full-tilt nonstop, and when we begin to rest, everything from our own soul to the fabric of society begins to breathe a sigh of relief. In the wise words of PBS Kids' Daniel Tiger, "Rest is best." In the even wiser words of Jesus, "The Sabbath was made for humankind."[48]

This is where playfulness begins.

ACCEPT THE INVITATION
Rest Well

1. Read Exodus 20:8-11. What is the significance of the Sabbath's inclusion in the Ten Commandments? Why do we so often treat this holy rest as optional?

2. Have you ever incorporated a regular Sabbath practice into your week? Why or why not? How might God be calling you into a repeated pattern of rest?

3. Read Mark 2:23-28. What is the difference between the Sabbath being created for people and people being created for the Sabbath? Why does Jesus draw this distinction?

4. When do you feel most rested? When do you feel most joyful? Is there a connection between the two?

5. What is one small change you could make this week to begin accepting God's invitation to holy Sabbath rest?

2

Be a Kid Again

We don't stop playing because we grow old;
we grow old because we stop playing.
—GEORGE BERNARD SHAW

As a little girl, growing up in the northern woods of Wisconsin, I played in our yard with knobbly toads I found hopping around the ferns, content with only my kiddie pool and the shaggy, evergreen forest that surrounded me. I remember the smell of grass and earth, the white glow of the birches in the sun of late afternoon, the breeze stirring their leaves to flash and spin. My parents barely had two quarters to rub together, with my dad funneling everything they had into a fledgling business, but I never knew it. In the summers, it was all forests and toads. In the winters, I stomped around our tiny kitchen in purple Cabbage Patch snow boots singing Frosty the Snowman, eating raw cookie dough, and watching the snow fall while the white-tailed deer meandered around the yard. My parents read me library books and trotted out the same, worn game of Candyland, and we laughed and laughed.

Even in lean seasons, kids pick up quickly on rhythms of play. Often what parents remember as achingly stressful times, kids experienced as deeply joyful. Author Shawn Smucker shared the story of his preschool-aged son Leo who, weeks into their state's pandemic stay-at-home orders, responded not with frustration or fear but in the following way:

> After I helped him out and he washed his hands and we were leaving the bathroom, he looked up at me and said, in his most sincere voice, "Dad, I love this day."
>
> Why would he say that?
>
> Why wouldn't he say that? We have plenty of food. He's getting to spend time with the whole family, as much time as he wants. We go to the park. We play more games than usual. We're eating dinner together every single night. He has his own personal butt-wiper.
>
> *I love this day.*
>
> This day. This day of uncertainty and viruses and plunging markets and economic shadows and elections and books to sell and all of that.
>
> *I love this day.*[49]

No wonder Jesus invites us to come to him as children— unafraid, unashamed, and unencumbered by burdens that are out of their control anyway. In embracing our dependence on him, we are freed to live in the playful, trusting joy of belonging to him. There is a simplicity to this joy, not because it isn't weighty, but because it is so profoundly good and true. When we give ourselves permission to be kids again, playfulness abounds.

Tom Junod was a young journalist when *Esquire* assigned him a piece on Fred Rogers, the Presbyterian minister-turned-television-host who dedicated his life to teaching everyone he could about the importance of this childlike posture toward ourselves, each other, and the divine. Writes Junod, "[Mr. Rogers] wanted us to remember what it was like to be a child so that he could talk to us; he wanted to talk to us so that we could remember what it was like to be a child. And he could talk to anyone, believing that if you remembered what it was like to be a child, you would remember that you were a child of God."[50] In the years since I'd outgrown my purple snow boots, my heart had lost my grasp on this truth—that I was, at my core, a child beloved by God and my life, and all its circumstances, rested squarely in his care. That each of us is held in just as tender a way. As I slowly began reawakening to this belovedness, a vital shift began to happen.

> PLAYFULNESS INVITES US TO TAKE DELIGHT IN THE MOMENT THAT'S RIGHT IN FRONT OF US, REMEMBERING THAT WE ARE LOVED. IT GIVES US PERMISSION TO BE SILLY, HAVE FUN, AND ENJOY SIMPLE PLEASURES.

It's hard not to live playfully when you know, deep down, how loved you are.

"Now" Time

Daryl and I planned our first vacation in seven and a half years with great anticipation. As my friend Beth likes to say, "Without kids, it's a vacation. With kids, it's only a trip." In the years since we became parents, we'd taken lots of trips—back to the Midwest for reunions with my family, up to Los Angeles to see Daryl's, and to a church camp in the San Bernardino National Forest, but we hadn't gone on a single *vacation*. To say we were a little bit excited would have been like saying Wayne Gretsky was a pretty good hockey player. I had been mentally packing my suitcase for six months. Any time work got stressful or the boys kicked a soccer ball through the living room or Felicity woke up before the sun, I'd mentally go to my happy place, a beach chair on a cruise ship with a lowbrow novel in my hand. My only real worry was how my stomach would look in my bathing suit and whether the cruise line served smoothies with those adorable tiny umbrellas because *I really wanted one.*

But our ship was set to sail on March 22... 2020. You see where this is going. Or rather, *not* going.

Instead of vacation, we received stay-at-home orders from the state of California. Not only were we not going to Mexico, we weren't going to Michael's craft store, either. Instead of feeling the ocean breeze ruffle my hair, my pixie cut grew into shaggy disarray as I juggled our oldest child's transition to distance learning, our middle child's virtual preschool sessions, and our youngest's daily snack-and-activity-and-diapering needs, the uphill climb of technology necessary to care for our congregation when we couldn't physically worship together, and my own burgeoning plague dread. It felt like a cosmic bait-and-switch; we'd been hoping for vacation bread and were given a pandemic stone instead.

We grieved our lost vacation and moved on as best we could, chugging along for a few more months as teacher-pastor-parents, sleeping little and playing even less, until one day I reached a breaking point.

"I don't think I can do this anymore," I told Daryl. "Apparently parenting and schooling our kids during a global pandemic isn't really a part-time gig."

"I don't know how we managed to do it as long as we did," he said.

After much prayer and soul-searching, together we came to a decision. I would transition down to one-quarter time at church, remaining in the pastoral mix but cutting way back on my responsibilities. We opted out of our school district's well-intentioned but often rocky distance learning and ordered a homeschool curriculum. For the first time in a decade, I stepped (mostly) out of the professional world. For the first time ever, and with much fear and trembling, I stepped into the world of (almost) full-time parenting.

The first days and weeks felt like a spin cycle in the washing machine as I tried to learn how to teach second grade and preschool simultaneously while caring for a rambunctious toddler to boot. As one friend helpfully noted, "There's not a first-year teacher out there who has an easy time of it." But brutal as the pandemic was, it also thrust me directly into beauty and the ache of *now* time. Suddenly I couldn't worry too much about next month or even next week; I was intimately tethered to the present moment, and whenever my attention would shift, another small person presented themselves for a snack or a snuggle or a school lesson.

As we grow, we begin to see ourselves on a timeline—the past, with its successes and regrets; the future, with its hopes and fears. This is necessary, of course. No one would ever start a retirement fund or stock up on Band-aids without a little foresight, and learning from the past is necessary to progress as people and as a culture.

IN OUR EFFORTS TO MAKE A LIVING, AS THEY SAY, MANY OF US HAVE CEASED TO MAKE A LIFE.

But all this pondering the past and fretting about the future can trap us, too. Our lives are lived right here and now, in this very moment. This is where children live—right here, right now. And this is the only place playfulness happens.

In *Pilgrim at Tinker Creek*, Annie Dillard writes of the importance of developing awareness of the blessings right in front of us. Often these delights are small—tiny, even. The question is, will we stop and listen, notice and accept them, and in this way receive the love of God? Or will we keep running at a breakneck speed, in a hurry to make our way through lives that require sacred pauses in order to be truly lived? Writes Dillard,

> The world is fairly studded and strewn with pennies cast broadside by a generous hand. But—and this is the point—who gets excited by a mere penny? But if you cultivate a healthy poverty and simplicity, so that finding a penny will literally make your day, then, since the world is in fact planted in pennies, you have with your poverty bought a lifetime of days.[51]

In our efforts to make a living, as they say, many of us have ceased to make a life. I know I didn't stop often for pennies. Who has the time? But this playful experiment had me asking, "What was I in such a gosh-darned hurry for, anyway?" Wasn't life ultimately about the pennies, after all?

Little by little, I started to embrace these simple opportunities, watching the children in my life for tips on how to live in now time. Dillard was right; pennies were everywhere! My eyes were simply untrained and my lifestyle too hurried. But with even a modicum of practice, my eyes started to focus and my steps to slow. Invitations to a deeper rhythm were everywhere. I watched my preschooler on the walk to the car. He paused to notice the dew on the grass. His eyes lifted to a crow flying overhead. He grinned when we came around the corner and he saw the new yellow bloom in his brother's flower bed. In thirty feet, he'd picked up three pennies. In the same thirty feet, had I not been watching him, all I'd have noticed was how late we were running.

Professor and poet Ross Gay set himself the challenge of writing one short reflection on delight every day as a spiritual exercise, situating himself squarely in now time. "[T]he discipline or practice of writing these essays occasioned a kind of delight radar," he wrote. "Or maybe it was more like the development of a delight muscle. Something that implies that the more you study delight, the more delight there is to study ... Which is to say, I felt my life to be more full of delight. Not without sorrow or fear or pain or loss. But more full of delight."[52]

> THE MORE I PLANTED MYSELF FIRMLY IN THE PRESENT, LIKE A CHILD, EYES AND HEART OPEN AND AWARE, THE MORE MY HAPPINESS BLOSSOMED.

One of the greatest gifts a child or a pet (or a poet!) can give is the reminder that this moment matters. We are invited to live instant-to-instant. Presently. Rooted in the seconds immediately before us. I was slowly discovering a similar thread to Ross Gay's; the more I planted myself firmly in the present, like a child, eyes and heart open and aware, the more my happiness blossomed.

One afternoon I put Wilson down for his nap, but Felicity wasn't quite ready for hers. With Lincoln reading on his own and Daryl holed up in the home office, it was just the two of us—a rarity in a family of five. I usually used these precious moments to clean the kitchen or put away the laundry, letting little Fizz tag along at my heels. But Annie Dillard had me thinking: what pennies were ready for the picking right now, in this moment?

A set of car keys or a mirror or a handful of dandelions can keep a baby happy for an hour. Felicity will often just sit still and watch her brothers go about their business (which is, of course, play), giggling to herself all the while. The world is a constant delight to her. If she could speak, it seems she might say, "Look, guys! The sun rose again! Look, everyone! Grass! Look, mom! BREAKFAST! AGAIN! IT'S AMAZING!"

Embracing this kind of wonder isn't childish, it's child-*like*: a mark of maturity, not immaturity. Jesus hits this note hard. When his disciples bicker over who will be greatest in the coming reign (a decidedly juvenile line of conversation), he tells them, "Unless you change and become like little children, you will never enter the kingdom."[53] The disciples' focus was on who could grab the most power; Jesus wanted them to see that power had nothing to do with it. It was about love.

"How can I love on you, baby girl?" I asked Felicity. She stared at me quizzically, her brow furrowed, her head tilted to the side. I'm convinced she'll be our earliest talker; she watches our mouths when we speak like she's trying to solve a mystery. *What are words, and how do I make them, too?* I set her down on the floor and perched nearby on the couch. She immediately scooted over and grabbed my knees, whimpering. I picked her up again. She arched her back and whined. I put her down. She grabbed my knees.

"Oh," I said. "Do you want me down by you?" I slid onto the floor. She wrapped her arms around my neck and did her happy dance, bouncing up and down on her little bare feet, drooling onto my shoulder. For the next twenty minutes she crawled over my legs, snuggled under my chin, scooted a few feet away and then back, pulled up to standing with my help, toddled a few steps, and then repeated it all again, overjoyed to have me all to herself, right down in her space. We tousled and laughed; I sang to her, and she cooed. When she grew tired, I scooped her up for her nap, both of us better in tune with each other and rich with pennies.

> CHILDREN ARE SOME OF OUR BEST TEACHERS OF ALL.

Now time can be this simple—and children are some of our best teachers of all.

Good Medicine

Kids can be a conduit for joy: particularly for those who aren't already caring for children on a daily basis. Our church serves an assisted living facility right across the street, and nothing lights up the residents there like a child. Youthful joy is a beautiful gift. It isn't just older folks who benefit from being with children, though. One of our most beloved babysitters occasionally texts me to ask if she can come over to snuggle our kids.

"No offense," she once told me, "but holding your baby is better than a therapy dog." Perhaps nothing helps us learn how to accept the invitation to be a kid again better than being in the presence of children.

A couple of years ago, I went to a doctor's visit with a friend. She was facing a scary diagnosis and needed some distraction, so we drove to Los Angeles together: her and me and then-eighteen-month-old Wilson. When she was called back for her appointment, he and I stayed out in the waiting area, passing the time. He quickly grew tired of the few board books I'd stashed in his stroller and squirmed out of my arms to roam the room.

My friend's doctor shared her waiting area with a chronic pain clinic. An elderly man and his wife sat a few chairs over from Wilson and me, her body frail and still, each small movement clearly causing her anguish. I did my best to keep Wilson away from them; he was at that veer-and-crash stage of toddlerdom when kids reel around like drunken sailors on stormy seas. Plus, he was a particular bruiser of a child, more likely to run a person over than to stop short.

But toddlers be toddlerin', and before I could stop him, he grabbed a small, yellow Nerf ball from his stroller and walked over to the man. Wilson studied him for a second, taking in his weathered, wrinkled skin, his pristine gray fedora, and his vacant expression. Then Wilson presented him with the ball, palm up, with a grin. I held my breath, ready to intervene and apologize.

Silently the man lifted the ball from Wilson's outstretched hand, placed it on the curved arm of his chair, and gave it a nudge. It rolled down the curve and bounced to the ground at Wilson's feet. Wilson's mouth fell open wide. Eyes alight, he grabbed the ball from the floor and presented it again. The man's downturned mouth flipped into a smile.

For the next twenty minutes, Wilson and the man played ball in the waiting room without speaking a word: rolling the ball, balancing it, giggling together when it bounced under a chair. The other people waiting for their appointments watched and smiled. The mood in the room lightened. Suddenly we were all together in this game—the two who played and the rest of us as spectators, co-conspirators instead of strangers. Wilson and the man played until the man's wife was called in for her appointment. When they rose to go in—the wife leaning heavily on her husband's arm, moving gingerly, each step a struggle— the man paused to lean down to Wilson and tip his hat.

"Thank you," I whispered. He nodded to me with a smile, and then they were gone.

Wilson returned to me and curled up in my lap, ready now for a story and a snuggle, the ball gripped firmly in his little hand, unaware of the joy he'd ministered to everyone in that waiting room, the permission he'd given each of us to play.

Creative Like Kids

Playfulness opens us to growth, discovery, innovation, and transformation. Many of the world's greatest thinkers approach questions and problems as opportunities for discovery rather than grave conundrums. "This World is not Conclusion," wrote Emily Dickinson.[54] Scientist Mary Budd Rowe tells the story of a school trip when she encountered perhaps America's most famous scientist of all time:

It was a strange sight: a man, standing before a fountain, watching the falling water and tilting his head from side to side. Drawing closer, I saw he was rapidly moving the fingers of his right hand up and down in front of his face. I was in seventh grade, visiting Princeton University with my science class, and the man at the fountain was Albert Einstein. For several minutes, he continued silently flicking his fingers. Then he turned and asked, "Can you do it? Can you see the individual drops?" Copying him, I spread my fingers and moved them up and down before my eyes. Suddenly the fountain's stream seemed to freeze into individual droplets. For some time, the two of us stood there perfecting our strobe technique. Then, as the professor turned to leave, he looked me in the eye and said, "Never forget that science is just that kind of exploring and fun." Nearly half a century later,

I've spent an entire career trying to impart Einstein's words to adults and children all over the world: Science is exploring, and exploring is fun.[55]

It's no coincidence that many of the world's most creative innovators have embraced childlike play. Steve Jobs dropped out of school; Marie Curie read so voraciously she often forgot to eat; James Baldwin loved the theater; Stephen King played the guitar in the Rock Bottom Remainders (a band made up of published authors including Dave Barry, Barbara Kingsolver, and Matt Groening). When speech therapist Lionel Logue helped King George VI overcome his stuttering—a true story dramatized in the 2010 movie *The King's Speech*—he didn't ask him to attack the problem head-on but instead to approach it playfully, employing creative strategies such as singing, chanting, and background noise in order to disrupt the king's anxious patterns. As anyone who's dealt with a speech problem knows, simply trying to overcome it rarely, if ever, works. With public speaking, as with so many other areas of our lives, addressing problems playfully is often just the ticket.

One of my favorite exercises when I lead speaking events is to invite participants to make a paper airplane. My request is often met with eye rolls or sighs, the slightly-more-adult version of a teenager's "But I'm too *old* for this!" I hand out sheets of paper and give quick instructions, and most folks eventually comply once the peer pressure in the room builds to a pitch and my implacable cheerfulness isn't punctured by their grumpitude.

"I'm giving you permission," I say. "Go for it."

Together we make paper planes and then I ask them to blunt the points (don't want anyone losing an eyeball) and we sail them around the room. The release is immediate. Smiles. Laughter. Exclamations over whose went farthest and whose landed in a centerpiece and whose did a loop-the-loop and came right back to its original launcher.

When we sit again to continue the presentation, we are altered. Lighter. Freer. More open to the work God has before us. It's such a silly, simple little thing, really: a paper airplane. And yet it contains almost infinite possibility for delight. Let's not let children have *all* the fun.

Playfulness is faithful to work on us if we let it, helping us to grow up by returning to childlike ways. Writes Simon Tugwell, "[Humans] can now only grow up properly by a painful dismantling of [their] false grownupness. To this end, the Son of God 'came to be a child with us,' so that we could be traced back to childhood and then grow up again, this time in a true way, till we come to the full stature of Christ himself."[56] Jesus leads the way into whimsy. In the Gospels, he is not focused on his own stature or reputation. Like a child, he sees what is valuable and important—God and

> PLAYFULNESS IS FAITHFUL TO WORK ON US IF WE LET IT, HELPING US TO GROW UP BY RETURNING TO CHILDLIKE WAYS.

people—and isn't concerned with wealth, power, or status, except in how they might hinder the faith and obedience of those to whom he ministers. While those around him jockey for position, Jesus speaks truth, brings healing, breaks chains, and welcomes children.

If you haven't felt the release of playfulness lately, invitations to it are right in front of you. Put this book down and go outside. Find a leaf, a lizard, a ladybug. Give yourself permission to be still for a few moments and watch the clouds overhead or the day's particular shade of blue or gray. If you can't get outside, check out your thumbprint—unique among some eight billion people. Listen to the sound of your heart. Make a paper airplane and give it a toss. Invitations to play are all around. Kids are experts at spotting them. We can learn again.

Free to Play

My childhood was largely filled by wandering in forests and snowbanks, baking and crafting and creating masterpieces with paint or markers or modeling clay. I read absolutely everything I could get my hands on, including cereal boxes and shampoo bottles. My parents drove my sisters and me to soccer games and hockey practice and enrolled us in piano lessons and took us on some epic trips, but they also just let us be. A lot. It was glorious. Many of my best memories involve slow afternoons when I'd be free to putter about with a stack of books, a tin of colored pencils, a bin of Legos, or some butter, sugar, and eggs while Mom prepped dinner or worked in the garden. In the summer, I swam in the lake. In winter, I read, begged my mom for access to her glue gun and sewing scissors, and watched falling snow landing soft and feathery or wet and heavy. There was space to breathe, to create, to ponder, to dream. One of our great modern tragedies is

LISTEN TO THE SOUND OF YOUR HEART. MAKE A PAPER AIRPLANE AND GIVE IT A TOSS.

that this is generally not how childhood works anymore. It's bad enough that we adults struggle to embrace playfulness; we now struggle to let even our *children* embrace childlike play.

Pamela Paul, author of *Parenting, Inc.* notes that for today's kids, "Every spare moment is to be optimized, maximized, driven toward a goal."[57] There is little room for free play or the creativity that arises when there is space enough to reflect and dream. As Claire Cain Miller wrote in "The Relentlessness of Modern Parenting," parents believe that "children who were bored after school should be enrolled in extracurricular activities, and that parents who were busy should stop their task and draw with their children if asked."[58] I live in Orange County, California, one of the parenting-pressure capitals of the western world, where child enrichment activities are as ubiquitous as traffic jams and kale smoothies. Our family regularly seeks to integrate free play not just into our children's lives but into our adult ones as well. But it's countercultural, to be sure. When I mention to people that one of our family values is allowing our kids to be bored, I get audible gasps. How *dare* we!

But the commercialized, pressure-filled culture of the day is unhealthy for both parents and children. Notes David Elkind, "Hyperparenting, overprotection, and overprogramming interfere with the healthy interaction of play, love, and work, and with the learning that accompanies their interplay."[59]

FREEDOM AND DISCOVERY ARE WONDERFUL FUELS FOR HAPPINESS. SOMETIMES SPACE AND SILENCE ARE THE BEST TEACHERS OF ALL.

Peter Gray notes that the most successful childhood play is self-chosen and self-directed and that "free play is also nature's means of helping children discover what they love."[60] Without the opportunity to explore their world and notice what piques their interest, children can grow up stunted, like a plant kept in a dark room. Kids require lots of space and time to make messes, try new things, and experiment with their environment. Offering unstructured time to our children is one of the greatest gifts we can give them.

This can be difficult, of course, both because it is becoming quite countercultural to not either put our children into constant enrichment activities or allow constant screen time, *and* because children with unstructured time often make big messes and get into quarrels with one another. As a parent,

I struggle to be patient with either of these things, but I also know that even the messes and the quarrels are teachers of one kind or another. When the pandemic hit and we faced weeks (and then *months*) of stay at home guidelines, we all had to give in to the mundane beauty of the same old things, day after day. We struggled mightily, but then we slowly, and sometimes painfully, began to discover new appreciation for what we already had and new appetites for creative play.

"I'm turning into you," I told my mom one day over a video chat, holding an egg carton and a paper towel tube up to the screen. "I'm saving garbage for the kids. And you were totally right—they love playing with it."

We don't need to cram managed activities into our children's every waking hour or to entertain these precious years away with television and apps. (Though both television and apps can certainly be a saving grace from time to time—no shame there!) And here's the wider lesson, applicable to parents and non-parents alike: we mustn't cram managed activities into *our* every waking hour or entertain our lives away with television and apps. Freedom and discovery are wonderful fuels for happiness. Sometimes space and silence are the best teachers of all.

What is it that you loved to do when you were a child? What brought you joy in your earliest years? Perhaps you can welcome that activity back into your life today. Pick up a new journal, join a soccer league, paint a picture, or fly a kite. After

I mentioned how much I'd loved riding horses as a kid, Daryl encouraged me to take lessons again. I rode my first Tennessee Walking Horse a few weeks later, and the little six-pack of lessons we purchased infused joy for weeks.

As we accept the playful invitation to be a kid again—giving ourselves permission be discoverers of the world, in touch with the holy present—happiness arrives at our fingertips. We begin to drink from the "river of delights" of which the psalmist writes.[61]

Let us never forget God's invitation to us to come to him as little children, open to love and wonder. Open to joy.

Perhaps it's time to make that paper airplane?

ACCEPT THE INVITATION
Be a Kid Again

1. Read Matthew 18:1–5. Why does Jesus tell his disciples—warring over who will be most important—that they must become "like a little child" in order to enter God's kingdom? What are children like? In what ways does God call us to become more like them?

2. What did you do for fun as a child? Which of these activities—if any—do you still enjoy as an adult? Are there any that you could incorporate into your adult life? What's stopping you?

3. Are there any children you interact with regularly (your own, or those of others)? How do they add joy to your life? How can you receive this joy more readily? If you don't regularly interact with children, is there a way God might be calling you into relationship with a child?

4. Children live in "now time," but adults are often burdened by past failures or future concerns. How can you plant your feet more firmly in the present?

5. Children regularly engage in free play, one of the simplest and most life-giving forms of playfulness. What is one way you can incorporate more free play into your everyday life?

3

Connect

Laughter, song, and dance ... remind us of the one thing that truly matters when we are searching for comfort, celebration, inspiration, or healing: We are not alone.

—BRENÉ BROWN

The sun burned brightly overhead, shimmering on Lake Michigan's blue-green waves as they rolled up the beach. My boys squirmed in the sand, dancing impatiently while I shellacked them in SPF 50, then running, full-tilt and shrieking, into the breakers.

After applying my own coat of sunscreen, I followed them, pausing only briefly to ponder why I'd chosen the widest-brimmed hat at the store before our trip, even though it looked *beyond* dorky. Some women look chic and glamorous in big hats. I look like Gilligan. But facing a choice between dorky now or possible skin cancer later, I chose dorky. Ah, late thirties, indignity is thy name.

I followed the boys into the waves, the water surprisingly chilly for late July. Lincoln turned to me with a grin and kicked the water, sending a splash cascading up my legs.

"No, *thank you*," I yelled, shrinking back into the shallows. His face fell, and he turned his back to me, aiming his splashes out to deeper water instead. My heart hiccupped. The day before, we'd spent fourteen hours in transit, flown across eight states, hauled suitcases in and out of cars and vans, and slept in unfamiliar beds. Lincoln had behaved beyond his years, helping schlep his brother's stuffed lamb and comforting his sister when her ears bothered her on the plane. He'd asked us for nothing the entire day, except help with his headphones so he could watch a Pixar film in the air, and permission to have a Sprite *just this once*. And now we were at the beach—*finally*, at last—and I'd rebuffed his first attempt at play. That splash was a six-year-old's request to share a little fun: a young boy's version of "I love you, Mom! Join me in this joy!" and I'd slammed it down. Also, I need not mention that he splashed me while I was *standing in the water wearing my swimsuit*. I mean, *come on*.

Play attempts are tender things. Kids or teens or fellow adults reach out with tentative but open hearts, asking, "Are you in? Can I trust you? Will you come along with me?" We can welcome these attempts, diving into the playfulness alongside them, or we can redirect, ignore, block, or—worst of all—reject them forcefully. The choice is ours, and the consequences are significant.

Often play attempts look like pure inconvenience. For example, our younger son loves snatching things. His vocabulary isn't very advanced yet, but he loves games. So when he grabs the book I'm reading, or Daryl's spatula during dinner prep, or big brother's homework, he's inviting us, clear as day, to play. The same is true of the baby when she makes her silly sounds, blowing raspberries and popping like a cork. She's asking if we see and hear her: if we want to play, too.

Rebuffing a play attempt isn't fatal, of course. At times it's necessary. I can't let Wilson snatch my hot coffee. I can't make eye contact with the baby while I'm driving. Not to mention the fact that sometimes we do actually need to be on time and therefore can't stop to investigate every leaf between the front door and the car. But shutting down play attempts repeatedly can wear away trust and connection. If we rebuff them as a general rule, those invitations will come less and less frequently, and eventually not at all. And when play grows absent, a relationship is almost always altered for the worse, with avenues to joy and connection closed down and trust all but destroyed.

In a study on marriage, John Gottman found that the one thing that predicted a marriage's longevity and success was how often partners made or positively responded to *repair attempts*—one person's effort to reconcile after a disagreement, friction, or conflict. After a fight, when a wife made a joke, did her husband laugh? When a husband offered an embrace, did his wife reciprocate, or stiffen? The positive reception of a repair attempt is a sign of health and resilience.[62] Play attempts—and their reception—are very similar. And in the same way, they predict the success and longevity of trust and closeness in a relationship. Deep, healthy emotional connection is nearly impossible without play.

PLAYFULNESS INVITES US TO MAKE AND RECEIVE PLAY ATTEMPTS WITH OTHERS, SAYING YES TO JOINING IN.

I wish I could say I realized all this within seconds that day at the beach, that I apologized or splashed Lincoln right back, that we found each other and celebrated the first moments of vacation together with joy. But we didn't because *I* didn't. Lincoln splashed in the waves alone until his cousins—all of whom are playfulness champions— came down to join us. It was only later that day the moment returned to me for what it was. What it could have been.

Wilson is an includer. A sheepdog. His greatest joy is when everyone in our home is gathered in one place. He will seek out Daryl, me, or any visiting adults and try to draw us back to the herd, even if we're just trying to get five minutes' peace to use the bathroom. But on the days Daryl is at work, Lincoln at school, and the baby slumbering away for her nap, I'm all he's got.

After a few moments of idly watching me gather laundry or scrub dishes or send an email, his face will break into a

Cheshire cat smile. He'll grab me by the hand and lead me to wherever the next game begins.

"Yet's make a fort!" he told me one morning. "Just a yittle one. Over dere." While I'd been cleaning up breakfast, he managed to wrangle every single pillow and stuffed animal in the house into a tiny corner between the sofa and the wall. A laundry basket was his throne atop the pile.

"You can hold Minnie-a-Pooh," he told me. "I will have Ee-whore and da whale. Sit dere." (We've tried to correct his pronunciation of poor Eeyore many a time, but it just won't stick. Poor Ee-whore.) I hesitated, really wanting to tell Wilson that I wouldn't fit in that small space, that I'd probably break the laundry basket, that I really should finish cleaning up the oatmeal under the baby's highchair before the ants found it again. I wanted to say no, but John Gottman turned up kindly and immovably in the back of my mind. My eyes opened to see the wonder brimming from Wilson's sparkling eyes. A childlike play attempt was on offer right here, right now, from my own beloved child. How would I respond this time?

I crouched down next to Wilson.

"Minnie-the-Pooh is hungry," I said, leaning into the fort. "Do you have any honey?"

He grinned. And in that moment, I felt an inbreaking of childlike joy well up in my own soul, too.

Divine Connection

One of the things I love most about Jesus is that he's always there. In a world where it can take me days or weeks to connect in person with a friend, the availability of God seems like a luxury almost too good to be true. Yet, as Alicia Akins writes, God is so ready to respond to us that when we are still "mid-cry" he "inclines his ear to us."[63] The mercy and love of the God who is always at the ready to bend to his children floors me. Still, even with this knowledge, I am often moving too swiftly to sit still and talk with Jesus, and without this connection my soul begins to wilt. Jesus is present; but I am not present to him. And as Simon Tugwell writes, "one can only learn to keep company with someone by keeping company with them."[64] For years, I'd let the guilt-shame cycle of my repeated attempts and failures to do the World's Best and Most Lengthy Daily Devotions™ keep me from simply showing up with Jesus when I could and with what time I had. But over time I've learned that Jesus never receives us back with a wagging finger and rolled eyes. Instead, he welcomes us with love. With open arms.

Weeks when Daryl and I are flying by the seats of our pants—juggling church initiatives, or back-to-school season, or a book deadline—we often don't have time for a date or a long, extended chat into the night. I can't tell you how many evenings we sit next to each other on the couch, hoping for fellowship and connection, when instead one of us starts to doze off. Yet thirteen years of marriage have taught us not to let the best become the enemy of the good; even a few moments of genuine connection are food for our marriage and our souls. A lingering hug might not last more than thirty seconds, but it can make an outsized difference to our happiness.

The same is true of our connection with God. Jesus often hiked up a mountain to pray, giving his Father uninterrupted time. But this wasn't a daily occurrence. Jesus studied the Scriptures in great depth, but there were days he spent walking from town to town, far from the scrolls of the Temple. While taking chunks of dedicated time once in a while is fairly essential to our spiritual health, between these larger blocks of time, we can commune with God as we walk along the road, wait in line at the pharmacy, lie in bed at night, or rise to meet the day.

> JESUS NEVER RECEIVES US BACK WITH A WAGGING FINGER AND ROLLED EYES. INSTEAD, HE WELCOMES US WITH LOVE. WITH OPEN ARMS.

The more I lean into this hopeful connection, the more time I *want* to spend with Jesus. The more I seek to find him in the ins and outs of my day, speaking to him in the shower, contemplating him on my morning drive, pausing for prayer before a meal, asking a friend if she'd like prayer right then, in the moment, the more I find he's been right at my side all the while. Even a brief check-in with Jesus is a sip of living water and important reorientation for the task at hand.

Psalm 139 is a helpful reminder for all the times we can connect with God: when we sit, when we rise, when we go out, when we come home—in short, *always*. We are continually seen and loved by God; he is never *not* present to us. How freeing to remember the consistent, watchful eyes of the Savior, not waiting for us to make it to a magical recliner or sanctuary or kitchen table to meet with him, but instead accompanying us each step of the journey and every minute of the day. Don't get me wrong; regular prayer and deep study of Scripture and communal worship spaces are beautiful things, essential to the maturation of our faith. But we can also meet God each moment of our lives, no matter where we are. Waking up to that consistent connection is a game-changer. A soul-changer.

Joining In

After I'd emailed my friends a request to play with them— and heard crickets for a while, because apparently I'm not the only one who's forgotten how to play—the first invitation I received was from Dakota, a young coworker at church who asked me to join her fancy indoor cycling class. To be honest, I didn't really want to go. I'm not into the trendy Orange County workout scene, and sweating alongside two dozen size-0 women (spoiler alert: I am not a size 0) didn't appeal *at all*. But I'd learned a thing or two about rebuffing a play attempt.

Dakota was reaching out, responding to *my* request. I took a deep breath and emailed her back.

I figured I could probably handle this cycling class, since I already rode an exercise bike at the YMCA a few times each week. I love our local Y. It's filled with this beautiful mixture of retirees and moms and kids and dads and oddballs, very few of whom are there to project an Instagram-worthy image. One of my favorite regulars in the cycling room must be nearing her late seventies. She hangs a big pink plastic purse on her handlebars while she exercises. The instructor will call out for us to *push it harder*, and this lady just grins and keeps going at her own pace, as if to say, "I'm *here*, okay? *Relax*." I want to be just like her when I grow up.

But as Dakota walked me through registration for Full Psycle (yes, that's the correct spelling, and yes, it made the English-major parts of my brain want to die a little), I started to feel a little bit of trepidation. First of all, our instructor was named after a fruit and was a *Lululemon Ambassador*, which apparently did *not* mean she was in charge of diplomatic relations with a country built upon overpriced leggings, though I tried that joke. Secondly, the class was $22, and for that price I could afford to stay out of shape, thanks much. Finally, I had to reserve a seat as if I was taking the GRE or perhaps attending the opera. So far, none of this was fun.

My online registration informed me that Full Psycle was a lifestyle and a full body-mind-spirit experience, not just a workout. It also said that if I had questions, I could bring them to the "Psy Girls" at the front desk, and then ended with a required waiver. I skimmed that up until the point where it said—no joke—that if I *died*, Full Psycle would refund my representative the purchase price of my unused class or classes. I swallowed hard. At least if I kicked the bucket on the exercise bike, my children could claim my $22. Goody.

I loaded up my fanciest workout gear—off-brand leggings, an off-brand tank top, an off-brand sports bra, and two athletic socks that actually matched, which made me pretty proud since I normally just grab two from our unmatched sock bin and roll with them—in my gym bag (which, come to think of it, cost just a couple dollars more than the fee for the single class), filled up my off-brand water bottle, and prayed: *Dear Jesus, please don't let there be any cameras.*

Dakota and I drove together to Full Psycle, nestled in an upscale mall just a couple miles down the road from our church. We signed in, got our shoes, and made our way into the darkened studio where thirty-seven white, state-of-the-art exercise bikes were perched upon the black rubber-matted floor. The studio's logo glowed and spun on the wall above our heads, and techno music pumped from strategically-placed speakers. It smelled like essential oils and ambition and tight abs. I texted Daryl a short video, and he texted back: *We really need to talk about you sneaking off and joining a cult.*

"I usually sit in the front," Dakota told me, waving the instructor over.

"Thanks for *not* this time," I said. "I'm terrified enough."

Peach—who turned out to be really fantastically nice and fresh-facedly enthusiastic in the way young fitness instructors tend to be—adjusted my bike, brought me hand weights, and told me to enjoy the ride. Other participants filed in one or two at a time, most of them women, most of them in their twenties, all of them looking straight out of an online ad for a yoga retreat. Glowing skin, sculpted leggings, strappy sports bras, and long, thick hair pulled into topknots and side braids. I felt like a scruffy buffalo on a prairie filled with gazelles. But before I could fall into true existential angst, Peach hit the go button, and we were off.

The darkened lights went out completely, and the speaker volume rose to a screaming pitch, blasting hip hop, techno, and Peach's voice directly into my brain. I didn't want to act like an old lady, but my already fragile eardrums were on *fire*. I briefly plugged them with my fingers before finding a position on the bike—head turned to the left, right ear to the sky—that shielded my poor ears from the speaker directly over my shoulder.

The workout was *intense*. In the saddle, out of the saddle, hand weights, bike push-ups. The front desk had given me clip-in shoes, and now I understood why: we leaned left, we leaned right, we pumped our weights in the air and rode hands-free.

There was no clock in the room, but after what felt like three solid hours of cycling, Peach chirped, "That's the warm-up, guys! Now we can start the workout!" Sweat dripped off the end of my nose, snaked in rivulets over my collarbone, streamed down my back. The darkened studio glowed with red lights and then blue ones; the screens lit up with our progress. There were twenty-five of us, and I was in twenty-third place, then twenty-fourth. Peach encouraged the back row to race the front three, gave us goals for our RPMs (which made sense to me) and our power levels (which never did). My water bottle quickly emptied, and my legs began to burn. Clearly my YMCA cycling had been just a pleasure cruise, a bike in the park, a lark. This was *serious*. I watched the tiny girl on the bike in front of me in fascination, her legs tirelessly pumping, her French braids swinging back and forth like dual pendulums.

Forty-five minutes later—long, long, *long* minutes—the screens lit up with our rankings, and Peach counted down the last ten seconds.

"You did it!" she said. "Track your goals, track your progress. Make this workout your own. Thanks for coming to Full Psycle!"

Dakota grinned at me.

"How was it?"

"Well, that was the most... *intense*... workout I've had in quite a long time. Also, I'm stuck to my bike." She helped me unclip my shoes and showed me where to stash my hand weights. I wrung out my towel, and we headed to the car. She'd done incredibly well: cycled fast, kept up with every push-up and weight-lift and hill climb. Full Psycle wasn't going to be *my* lifestyle, but I could see why it was fun for her.

Beyond the pulverized calories, cycling with Dakota brought the two of us together. Playing together, I realized, can give us a glimpse into what makes another person tick. I'd known that Dakota could lead a great youth group event, but now I'd seen firsthand her joy in pushing her muscles to their limit. There was suddenly a new ease between us, a deeper connection, and I felt a new admiration for her grit and drive. Playfulness helps us connect; connecting with one another gives us greater freedom to play together.

> PLAYFULNESS HELPS US CONNECT; CONNECTING WITH ONE ANOTHER GIVES US GREATER FREEDOM TO PLAY TOGETHER.

Plus, I got to write up my playfully snarky take-down of the whole experience. Win-win.

Invitations to connect can arise spontaneously, like a splash at the beach. Other times, we may need to ask to be included, or reach out with a connection of our own. Offering a play attempt is a vulnerable thing, and our efforts to connect will sometimes be turned down. But rather than letting that discourage us, we can use those moments to help remind us to receive the play attempts of others with tenderness. A little connection can go a long way toward both our happiness and that of those connecting with us.

We were headed back to that same beach again this summer, until COVID derailed our plans. Now we sit together in the backyard, with a sprinkler made out of a hose and an old olive oil bottle, and Lincoln, with a glimmer in his eye, picks it up and heads toward me. I pause. Then I grin.

Look out, Lincoln. Mama's splashing back.

ACCEPT THE INVITATION

Connect

1. Read John 13:34-35. What is the tie between love and connection? How does loving someone well include connecting with them? How does God connect with you?

2. Can you think of an instance when you offered a play attempt and it was rebuffed? What was that experience like for you?

3. Can you think of an instance when you rebuffed the play attempt of another? What was that experience like?

4. What feelings arise in you when you are well-connected to someone? How do you keep this connection strong?

5. Who is someone with whom you wish you had a deeper connection? What is one thing you could try this week to establish or strengthen that connection?

4

Improvise

Improvisation is too good to leave to chance.
—PAUL SIMON

Twitter suggested I take an improv class, which seemed as good a next step into the land of happiness and delight as any. But to be honest, my serious side struggled with even the idea of taking a class of this kind. There is nowhere to hide in improv! I'd have to put myself all the way out there in a room filled with complete strangers to pick up whatever characters and scenarios they laid down. I hadn't done improv since my short stint in community theater back in Wisconsin the better part of a decade earlier. There, I'd turned to the stage as a way of staving off the stir-craziness of a particularly nasty Wisconsin winter. It—both the improv and the winter—hadn't gone well.

I planned to go alone and probably even give a fake name—yes, really—to further curtail the possibility of public humiliation. That plan failed when Daryl saw it on my calendar.

"Can I come?" he asked.

"You're kidding," I said. Daryl freezes when we go off-script with the church announcements. While opening a birthday present, he will literally announce to the entire room, "Just so you all know, my *face* probably won't *look* happy. That doesn't mean I don't like this present. I'm just not very good at spontaneous joy."

But he wasn't kidding. He really wanted to go. Parenthood and pastoring have both helped him learn to flow with the rhythms of kids and kingdom. It's been a beautiful shift to witness, though it still surprises me from time to time.

So we hired a babysitter, kissed our kids goodbye, and soon found ourselves climbing the stairs above a bowling alley, paying $10 apiece for what I was pretty darned certain would be a class in communal indignity.

PLAYFULNESS INVITES US TO ENGAGE IN SPONTANEITY AND DISCOVERY, HANG LOOSE, GO WITH THE FLOW, AND THINK ON OUR FEET, SAYING "YES, AND ..."

Fifteen of us gathered in a conference room, its walls lined with royal-blue-striped wallpaper shabby with age, its simple black platform stage roughly the size of a one-car garage. Our instructor, Andrew, gave us a short pep talk, telling us that there were no mistakes in improv, that when anyone on stage with us introduced a new element we were to go with it, to accept it into the world of our scene.

"We don't say no here," said Andrew. "We say *yes, and…*"

Daryl, who often gets nervous writing emails, sat beside me cool as a cucumber. After thirteen years of marriage, I still couldn't figure this guy out.

Our first warm-up involved animal sounds; our second was called "loser ball."

"I'm going to be *really* good at this one," I whispered to Daryl.

One man left after the first five minutes.

"Where's James?" Andrew asked.

"Oh, he always does this," a classmate answered. "It's part of his schtick."

"Y'all are paying up front next time," said Andrew, who'd told us we could give him our $10 at the mid-class break.

We lined up to practice partnered vignettes, each person randomly paired with another and then another. We spun through scenes at a rapid-fire pace, the class erupting in laughter before falling silent to watch the next act. A heavily muscled man in a gray T-shirt introduced a stakeout. A woman in her forties found an abandoned baby in a pumpkin patch. An older gentleman took off his shoes and cawed like a crow. A Swiss woman pretended to get naked in a dark alley.

"I'm European," she said. "You know how we are."

A big guy pretended to be a sound effects voice actor and elaborated upon all the different types of explosions he could do—while in an airport scene. Daryl tried to get to the bottom of why his basketball teammate had a torn ACL but wouldn't go to the doctor. I stalked an ex-boyfriend through an art gallery. An older couple pretended to be brother and sister deep below the ocean in a nuclear submarine.

"Just because you are nine months older doesn't mean you can boss me around down here," the woman said.

"I'm not bossing you around because I'm *older*, I'm bossing you around because I'm *the captain*," the man said.

There was a good deal of profanity and an absolute cavalcade of laughter.

With no time to muddle over what to say or how to say it, where I should take a scene next, or how my classmates were perceiving me, there was only presence, reaction, engagement, whimsy. I was playing—*really playing*—in a way I hadn't since childhood. Suddenly I was on a Ferris wheel talking to a man in his twenties about his dead mother (cotton candy always reminded him of her). A minute later I was complaining about a preschool classmate's smelly stick pony. Andrew warned us away from outlandish absurdity—"The funniest bits are those about normal life," he said.

It was true. In the scene on the military submarine, loading the torpedoes didn't grip us; the drama between a brother and sister did. We accepted ideas from one another as gifts, joined each other in play, reserved criticism, and simply entered in.

The only person who seemed *not* to be having a good time—besides James, who we never did see again—was a woman who snuck in late and then kept trying to refuse participation.

"I'm bad at this," she said. "I don't know what to do." She stopped every scene to ask for directions or instructions. "Should I talk to him?" she asked Andrew, pointing to her partner who kept stealing food from the organic farmer's market in their scene, waiting for her to call him out on it. She couldn't find her way into playfulness and spontaneity, instead repeatedly asking things like, "Why does he keep calling me babe? I'm not his girlfriend."

When we don't feel safe or won't let ourselves enter into the moment, joy becomes elusive. I saw myself in this struggling woman—afraid to make a mistake, unwilling to give in to the exercise at hand. How often have my kids asked me to join them in play and instead I've offered commentary, peppered them with questions, or redirected them to something more serious when seriousness was not at all, in that moment, required? Just yesterday I was trying to get the baby to practice walking when all she wanted to do was chew on my necklace.

So much of the improv night was simply invitation and permission: the grace of being allowed to let loose. *You can be silly. You can go bananas. Pretend you're hang gliding, in surgery, at a football game, a bed and breakfast, an army boot camp. Say something ordinary and see where it takes you. Go ahead. We'll all come with you.*

Daryl stood in the middle of a circle of strangers and sang "Twinkle, Twinkle, Little Star." I belted out "I Will Survive," despite knowing only half the lyrics.

"Do you do corporate events?" I asked Andrew during a break. "Our church staff needs this."

Improv shook loose something in my soul that had been wound too tightly for years. Fun was... *fun.* Who knew? Thanks to a wise guide and a dozen other people willing to *go there*—to give ourselves and each other permission to be silly and imaginative and playful together—Daryl and I laughed more than we had in years. And it was all so beautifully uncomplicated. No props. No gadgets. Just people—nearly all of them strangers—ready to play.

The class helped me see how playfulness is inherently improvisational. We can adapt to what life throws at us begrudgingly, or we can say, "Yes, and..." Life is unscripted, after all, and often our own good intentions and unspoken expectations stop us short on the road to happiness. It's why Daryl and I almost always start family trips with a marital argument. It's why major holidays rarely live up to the hype. When we are weighed down with our own plans, it's not as easy to dance with the wild wind of the Holy Spirit. But when we lay hold of the invitation to live with open hands, we become more nimble, adaptable, and grace-filled. We are encouraged—by God, by life, by circumstance—to improvise.

Improv Jesus

Jesus was a great improviser. Sure, he was God and all, but he was also *fully human*. He only knew what the Father and the Spirit revealed to him. There were certainly instances when God revealed things to him in the moment, as he does with us. But Jesus did not walk into every single social situation with a prewritten script. Often we see him illustrating his preaching with whatever was nearby—a farmer's field, a coin, a mustard-seed-tree. He responded *in* the moment *to* the moment— seeing the person, the need, the hope, the fear. Following the leading of the Holy Spirit.

"The wind blows wherever it will," Jesus tells Nicodemus.[65]

We have much to learn from Jesus's adaptability, his "yes ... and"-ing. Life is filled with opportunities to playfully respond to the moment at hand. For example, anyone who works with teenagers is no stranger to improvisation. The spunk and whimsy of the meme-generation is not to be underestimated. They are wise and witty and hilarious and profoundly insightful. I'm regularly floored by how quickly our church's youth director is able to think on his feet.

"Happy birthday!" one teenager called out as Matt stood to begin the evening orientation on our annual winter youth trip. Matt paused for a beat.

"It is not my birthday," he said. "Not even close. But that brings me to tonight's topic: the schedule for the weekend!"

As we improvise, we learn how to respond rather than react, becoming part of the scene instead of trying to escape, deny, or alter it. We begin to see others as partners in the dance rather than adversaries. We become open to the movement of the Holy Spirit, the winds of change, the joy of the moment. Improvisation teaches us to live with open hearts, open eyes, and open hands; ready for anything, but committed to the one great principle of saying *yes, and* ... How often God is waiting to meet us in whatever follows that wonderfully loaded *and* ...!

After the improv class Daryl and I linked arms on our walk to the car.

"You were great in that garden scene," I told him.

"I never knew you killed a man," he said.

ACCEPT THE INVITATION
Improvise

1. Read Ruth 1:1–22. How does Ruth's life change? What is Ruth's response to this earth-shaking tragedy? What does she have to teach us about improvisation and following the Lord?

2. What's a minor inconvenience you've faced lately? What might that inconvenience have to teach you about improvising?

3. Free, spontaneous play can be a deep joy. How can you recognize and respond to spontaneous opportunities to play?

4. The woman who struggled the most in the improv class wouldn't allow herself to be vulnerable. How are vulnerability and joy connected? Where do you feel most comfortable being vulnerable? Least? When do you feel most joyful?

5

Do Useless Things

Every time I see an adult on a bicycle, I no longer despair for the future of the human race.

—H. G. WELLS

My friend Cara visited for a few days one summer, bringing her adorable, bright-eyed sons, whom my boys immediately adopted as their new best friends *evereverever*. We laughed and played in the hot California sun, and when they left for home—ten hours away—my kids were bereft.

"When will we ever see them again?" our oldest wailed.

On their way home, Cara texted me:

A little surprise is coming in the mail to you, and because Amazon might beat the thank you card I've yet to write, just know that this is something you'd probably never buy for yourself ... but y'all do hospitality like no other, and to me being hospitable means celebrating LIFE. So, this is something to help the whole family celebrate.

I couldn't imagine what she might be sending. A box of candy? A toy for the kids? (The boys had been *really* into playing with water guns together.) I joked that I hoped it was a robot-maid, like Rosie from the Jetsons. I suspected it was a book; Cara and I began as book-buddies, after all.

The box arrived, perfectly square and fairly light. I opened it with Daryl, and we looked uncertainly at its contents.

She'd sent us ... a disco ball.

"What on earth am I supposed to do with this?" I asked Daryl. He laughed.

"I think that's the point."

It was.

Everyone has a side hustle these days, or so it seems. Your sister makes wreaths. Your neighbor coaches soccer. Your pastor (ha!) writes books. We monetize our skills, sell our free time, invite our friends over for a party that's actually a sales pitch. But much is lost when we begin to commoditize everything from our hours to our friendships. We miss the joy of doing things simply because they bring us delight. So often happiness comes from small, simple acts that have no ultimate value

> PLAYFULNESS INVITES US TO PURSUE ACTIVITIES, HOBBIES, AND EXPERIENCES PURELY FOR THE JOY OF THEM.

except that they bring us the pleasurable release of play. Think of doing a jigsaw puzzle, picking a bouquet of wildflowers, riding a bike, watching a football game. Cotton candy has no nutritional value, but once a year at the state fair it can be the perfect snack. No one needs to wear accessories, but a great pocket square or a fun pair of earrings can help an outfit truly sing. Not to mention that, as the wise guru Winnie-the-Pooh once said, "Nobody can be uncheered with a balloon."[66]

Savoring the Good Stuff

Playfulness isn't utilitarian—that is, it's not useful, a means to an end. Instead, play opens up new connections in our minds and hearts *because* it is not purely transactional. The ultimate goal of play is... wait for it... *play*. When we begin to allow ourselves the occasional frivolity—whether that's going for a walk just because it's a beautiful day, snagging that new novel at the library for no other reason than we want to read it, or truly savoring a bite of food rather than eating hurriedly— we will begin to find ourselves in a happier state. Sure, we may be able to accomplish more if we speed through life and only pursue purposeful work; but at what cost? Who would we become?

Recently Daryl and I invited a ministry family from another church over for dinner. We did what we usually do with other pastors: we talked church, theirs and ours. We spoke about staffing needs and worship flow and organizational health and denominational politics. It was all perfectly fine. But then someone at the table asked, "What do you do for fun?" Eyes lit up. Smiles broke through. The entire tenor of the evening changed, and at the end of this little snippet of conversation, talking about gardening and writing and hiking, we had connected in a deeper way. There's drive—important for work and hustle, production and accomplishment—but then there's heart: important for everything else, and then some.

At the height of my career striving, a professor told me she was taking a sabbatical to help care for her grandchildren.

"Won't that hinder your publishing work?" I asked her. She laughed.

"Of course it will," she said. "But there's work and there's life, and life is always more important."

At our church's new members class, we ask people to share their faith stories, their denominational backgrounds, and what brought them to our church. But then we also ask what they love, and here is where the stories begin to spill out and people begin to unite with one another. Christ unites us, but when a person hears that the guy two chairs over *also* likes fly fishing? Well, there's a bond that can't be broken.

Nearly a decade ago, Daryl and I went to Paris. Before you picture us as glamorous jet-setters, I should mention that I was enormously pregnant with Lincoln, so the fancy things people usually go to Paris to enjoy—tartare, long walks along the Seine, nightlife—were not on the table. Soft cheeses and fine wine were straight up verboten. Or whatever the French word for verboten is.

We showed up at our friend Steven's achingly charming flat off Rue de la Lune, dropped our suitcases, and followed him out on a walking tour of the City of Lights. Steven had a Real Job with a Big Company, all grown up just a handful of years after we'd graduated together. His suits were tailored ("I have a guy," he told us); his shoes were shiny; his French was flawless. But for all that, he still managed to exude a deep, gentle kindness. I've met few people as hospitable as Steven.

"So," he told us as we strolled along the Seine, "I've made us a dinner reservation for tomorrow. One of the best restaurants in Paris. My treat." We thanked him but didn't process until later what "best restaurant in Paris" might actually mean. We were living in rural Wisconsin at the time. Our local *best restaurant* had fried fish on the menu and eight kinds of pie. If you added a drink and after-dinner coffee, it'd run you $24. Which is why we never went there and instead spent date nights at Red Robin because they had bottomless fries *and* bottomless root beer floats for under ten bucks.

That night, jet-lagged and awake at 3 am, we Googled the fancy-pants restaurant.

"No *way*," I said, dying a little inside. "Is that in *dollars*?"

"Worse," said Daryl. "It's in *euros*." I then died the rest of the way and had to be resurrected by Daryl shaking me and hissing, so as not to wake our kind host, "Court, he wants to take us. He is paying. *Take a breath.*"

My inability to spend money on anything isn't totally my fault; it's at least partly genetic. I come from frugal, Midwestern stock. My great-grandmother used to take half a sleeping pill to stretch her prescription and then wander the house at night, chatty and hallucinating. It freaked the heck out of us kids when she visited over the Christmas holidays and we'd wake to her standing over us, muttering about angels. My grandmother will reuse a teabag until it's no longer recognizable as a teabag. My mother has never shopped at the front of a store in her entire life because, of course, the sale racks are at the back. I cut my own hair, and *sometimes you can tell.*

ACTUAL TEXT CONVERSATION WITH A FRIEND DURING OUR STAY-AT-HOME ORDERS:

Friend: Who is cutting your hair?

Me: I am.

Friend: You learned to do that?

Me: Yes. About eight years ago.

Friend: ...

Me: I've been cutting it ever since.

Friend: ...

Me: Yes, I was this weird even before COVID.

This penchant for pinching pennies only got worse in seminary, when I worked every part-time job I could land, but our bank account was regularly in the red. Frugality can be a virtue, but the anxious money-management borne out of seasons of real poverty cuts deeply. By the time we graduated and began to make a little more money—enough to replace our threadbare jeans and holey shoes—my hands had tightened so firmly around our proverbial purse strings that I couldn't fathom spending an extra dollar on a luxury when a bargain-basement version would do. Daryl and I had more than one argument about brand name over-the-counter medication. He'd ask for NyQuil or Claritin, and I'd bring home Ye Olde Generic Version.

"This isn't what I wanted," he'd say.

"Yes, but it was two dollars less," I'd counter.

"But it also doesn't *work*," he'd say.

"That's all in your head," I'd tell him, watching him sniffle for days until he'd finally sneak off to the pharmacy on his own. Do you know what doesn't save any money? Buying the generic medication *and* the brand name one.

The real problem began when my frugality started to steal joy from those who want to bless us. Or when the penny-pinching had real-world consequences, because sometimes the cheapest version of a product or service actually doesn't work nearly as well or last nearly as long (sorry, Daryl). My mom knew this and tried to teach it to me when I was a girl. There were things we never scrimped on in our family. Things like good hiking boots and brand-name hockey skates. My mom's frugality was about saving money anywhere we could so we could invest it in other ways. Generic soccer shorts may have made me feel dorky, but they worked just as well, and we could put those saved dollars toward a road trip to Chicago to see Great-Grandma do some more midnight wandering. I didn't learn my mom's wise nuance well, though. I clung to my frugality, even when it didn't make sense. Even when it didn't have a higher purpose. Even when I wasn't being frugal on my own dime.

Enter: Paris.

After more middle-of-the-night whispering, Daryl agreed to talk to Steven to make sure he really *wanted* to take us to this Michelin-star-rated restaurant. Daryl is infinitely kind in those moments when he and I both know that I'm being a little unreasonable. It isn't that he won't push back—he pushes back *plenty*—it's that sometimes he knows that the fastest way to help remove the bee from my bonnet is to just address the issue head on.

By the time I awoke the next morning, the guys were in the kitchen drinking strong coffee and reminiscing about their old roommate days. The matter was settled. We were going, and Steven would treat.

I glammed up as best I could for someone who required knee-length black compression stockings and looked roughly fifteen months pregnant. (Was I, in fact, actually only six months pregnant? Yes. Did I, in fact, have to carry a doctor's note, so the airline would let me board even though I looked full term, due to the fact that Daryl and I produce giant, red-cheeked Midwestern babies? Yes again. Oh, the good times.) We slipped into a chic booth at the chic restaurant with Steven looking chic (as always) and Daryl doing a far better impression of chic than I could muster, and our courses began to arrive. You know what makes Michelin-starred food taste kind of like garbage? Guilt.

The food was sculptural and vibrant and ethereal and probably delicious, but I was too busy being grumpy because it cost nine billion euros and also, it was *tiny*. The second course was literally *a* ravioli.

"This is a fifty-eight-dollar ravioli," I whispered to Daryl while Steven was in the restroom. "I did the math." Daryl sighed, with a sigh that contained multitudes, and I knew even then that I needed to figure out how to enjoy this gift—how to be gracious about it, because it was not even my money and dining in such luxury was an experience I'd likely never have again—but then the third course came and disaster with it.

I have severe food sensitivities that I won't bore you with here (really, the only thing worse than talking about someone's food issues is discussing their skin rashes, and yeah, let's not), but despite all Steven's chatting with the chef beforehand, something in the third course was on my List of Death, and within minutes I was in severe gastrointestinal distress. I slipped quietly from the table and ran for the chic bathroom, which, being chic, was directly in the center of the restaurant—literally the size of a telephone booth—and featured *an open top*. That's right, whatever went on in there would be broadcast to the entire restaurant. And what was about to happen in there was not fit for public auditory consumption.

I returned to our table and grabbed Daryl's shoulder in that particular marital way that communicates *things are bad, boy, they are really, really bad right now*, smiled at Steven, and bolted.

Somehow I made it home without my guts exploding all over the sweaty Paris Metro, but it was quite a struggle, let me tell you. A feat of clenching. I then spent the next three days alternating between Steven's adorable Parisian bathroom and our pull-out bed while Daryl saw the Louvre and the Eiffel Tower and the Arc du Triomphe and came home every night with digital photos to tell me about all the culture I was missing.

Though I *did* make it through the entire season of *Survivor: China* in the pull-out bed, so it's not like I wasn't getting *any* culture.

Essential Non-Essentials

Telling ourselves—or anyone else—that playfulness is *required* is a bit like Jane Austen's arranged marriages in her novels. There's a chance it might work out well, but a much bigger chance that the parties involved will find themselves uncomfortable, bound out of obligation, and quite miserable as a result. Instead of a requirement, I've found it most helpful to think of the playfulness as an *invitation*. Play extends a hand to us, inviting us to let go of our unhealthy seriousness for a newer, fresher perspective. Playfulness is good in part *because* it isn't necessary, forced, or required.

This permission is joyful, but it can be painful, too. Embracing whimsy means we have to let go of our unhealthy fixation with always being Practical Adults™ doing Practical Adult Things™. Even I could see that sometimes my frugality was a sign of character and thoughtfulness, but at still other times it was a pattern of stubborn sin that dishonored those who were trying to bless me or, worse yet, caused me to be stingy instead of generous and kind. Scripture speaks of the importance of being wise stewards of our money, but also of the joy of drinking deeply, giving to others, embracing blessing, and savoring what is good.

Jesus was a master-celebrator. He feasted so often that his harshest critics basically called him a wino. These same folks criticized John the Baptist for being too serious about the spiritual discipline of fasting. (You really can't win with some people, can you?) Yet Jesus wasn't one to let this sort of hypocrisy lie. He called out the crowd on their inconsistency: "John came fasting and they called him crazy," Jesus said. "I came feasting and they called me a lush, a friend of the riffraff. Opinion polls don't count for much, do they?"[67]

In Matthew 26, a woman anoints Jesus with expensive perfume. Rather than chastise her—as the disciples are tempted to do—he celebrates the overabundance of her gift. "Wherever the gospel is preached throughout the world," he says, "what she has done will also be told, in memory of her."[68]

Isn't this what worship is? Giving Jesus our all, knowing that he has and does and will continue to give us *his*?

> EMBRACING WHIMSY MEANS WE HAVE TO LET GO OF OUR UNHEALTHY FIXATION WITH ALWAYS BEING PRACTICAL ADULTS™ DOING PRACTICAL ADULT THINGS™.

It is significant that Jesus' first miracle was not a physical healing or the casting out of a demon: things that were essential to the physical and mental flourishing of those who were suffering. He would go on to do those things frequently, but his inaugural, divine act of mercy was to help a bride's family avoid awkwardness at a wedding. They'd run out of wine, and this would not stand! I'm guessing there was a person or two at that wedding in need of physical healing, too, but this is not how Jesus chooses to begin the miraculous season of his ministry.

"They have no more wine," Mary, his mother, tells him.

The importance of this beverage at a first-century wedding cannot be overstated. Guests needed to quench their thirst, of course, but even more than that, wedding wine was a sign of hospitality, welcome, and honor. Running out of it would be a bit like running out of chairs at a fancy, sit-down dinner today. A few people might awkwardly bend over and try to eat their food, but most would leave feeling quite insulted. Good wine was about celebration, but it was also a sign of caring for the guests as members of an extended social family.

Yet the wine was also *not* an absolute, essential physical need. No one was going to *die* without wine at that wedding. In the hierarchy of needs, surely a physical healing would have been more *essential*, right? But Jesus performs his first miracle over large jars of water, turning them into wine. And not just wine, but *really, really good wine.*

"You have saved the best till now!" the master of the banquet crows.[69] The sheer generosity, the absolute abundance, the unnecessary, over-the-top grace speaks volumes about how God loves us. Sometimes the most "useless" things are also the most significant.

You could even say he has a flair for the miraculous, that Jesus.

Dining Anew

Fast forward nearly a decade, and mid-playfulness-experiment Daryl and I were invited to a friend's surprise fortieth birthday dinner at the fanciest restaurant in Orange County. The husband of the birthday girl even called ahead to make sure they could prepare food that'd be totally safe for me. I couldn't wait to celebrate with them. But then I looked up the prices.

"They're treating," Daryl said. "This is a birthday party." He paused and then said that thing that all spouses need to say to one another from time to time: "This is not about you."

I pondered encountering another $58 ravioli, of trying to enjoy a dinner more expensive than our most recent vehicle purchase. (That SUV was *very* used, but still.) A meal like this seemed so frivolous. So silly. So … special? Yes, that was it. Our friends wanted to celebrate this milestone birthday around a table with gorgeous food. They wanted to make a memory with those nearest and dearest to them at a table overlooking the ocean. I thought about all the ways they were incredibly generous with God's blessings—from tithing to our church to being two of the most thoughtful gift-givers I've ever encountered.

I turned Daryl's words over and over in my mind. It was *not* about me, except that they'd chosen to include me in their joyful celebration, inviting me to a table I'd never sit at on my own. Could I swallow my pride and self-righteousness and enjoy this meal? I was determined to try.

Days later, we sat at a table overlooking the Pacific swells with four other couples, tasting tiny portions of beautiful, frivolous food—which, I was unsurprised to discover, went down much more smoothly when eaten with an open mind and an open heart. As I sat there, surrounded by friends, the ocean waves crashing onto the rocks below, I realized there was a great opportunity before me to get off my high horse, where I had been really quite stuck, and accept the gift of the banquet before me. To surrender to joy. To lay hold of delight.

Turns out playfulness and savoring are a perfect pairing.

A Last Taste

My great-grandmother lived for eighty years in a two-story brownstone a handful of blocks from Chicago's Wrigley Field. *Spunky* doesn't begin to describe her. At ninety years of age, when it became apparent she needed heart bypass surgery, doctor after doctor turned her down.

"You're ninety!" they'd say. "That surgery is risky on someone decades younger than you!" Undeterred, she finally found a doctor who agreed to do it, advising her that *if* she recovered from the surgery, it'd offer her three or four years at best. It ended up buying her thirteen more.

Though we only visited her once or twice a year, the trips always left an impression. She was always, *always* in her pajamas. (Truly I am a woman after her own heart.) We played cards, ate pastries, lost to her in Scrabble.

"That's not a word," my dad would say.

"Look it up," she'd tell him with a grin.

The last time I visited her, she'd been moved to an assisted living facility in the suburbs for her final Christmas. She'd told everyone for decades that if we moved her from her home, she'd die. Though at age 102, nearly deaf and with failing eyesight and limited mobility, she could no longer care for herself, my heart ached knowing she would leave this earth far from her beloved bay window overlooking Lakeview's Cornelia Street.

By the time I arrived at her room, fresh from seminary exams, she was unresponsive, her thin frame nestled in a hospital chair, her eyes closed. I said hello and held her hand, swabbing the inside of her mouth with medical sponges to moisten its parched sides. Her eyes remained closed and her hand didn't respond to my squeeze, but still I talked to her, telling her about school and our travels, about

OUR WORLD IS FILLED WITH USELESS ACTIVITIES THAT CAN FILL US WITH ABSOLUTE DELIGHT.

Daryl and our hopes for the future. No response. Then I mentioned I'd visited the Fanny Mae candy store.

Suddenly, Gram's head gave a jerk. Her eyelids fluttered, then rested again.

"Do you ..." I paused. "Do you want some chocolate?" She moaned, softly.

This was before all my hospital chaplaincy training where I would learn about swallow tests and the importance of asking a patient's nurse whether they can have solid food or if they were in danger of choking. Knowing what I know now, I'd never do what I did then. I dug into my bag, opened the white box of Gram's favorite chocolates, and pulled out a dark raspberry cream. I held it to her lips. They parted.

"MMMMMMMM!" she grunted, loudly and smackingly chewing the candy, swallowing without a hint of distress. I held up another. A white-chocolate Trinidad.

"OMMMMMMMM!" she proclaimed, polishing it off. I held up a third. Her lips remained closed. She was sated. I returned my hands to hers, laughing and crying with the small act of grace God and Grammie had allowed me to witness. She died two days later, Fanny Mae her final meal.

I only hope I meet my end with the taste of chocolate still on my tongue.

Our world is filled with useless activities that can fill us with absolute delight. And many of them are so very simple. Take a breath, take a pause, take a taste. Smell the herbs. Look into the eyes of the friend. Snuggle the baby. Watch the snow fall. Each of these things serves no grand purpose. But each one changes us, incrementally transforming overly serious minds into open ones and stubborn hearts into joy-filled ones. The floor *needs* scrubbing, but is there actually something even more needful right in front of you? Pausing a full moment to hug the living being before you—the spouse, the child, the parent, the friend, the fluffy dog—may be even more needed.

Noticing your breath might just change your soul. Playing that board game could kick-start a friendship. And who doesn't like a sweet treat from time to time—empty calories or no?

Perhaps the "useless" things are the most essential of all. Give yourself permission to do useless things. Do them often.

Then watch the joy roll in.

ACCEPT THE INVITATION
Do Useless Things

1. Read Ecclesiastes 5:19–20. We often think of enjoying life as a frivolous pursuit, but here Scripture seems to encourage it. What does savoring "useless things" teach us?

2. Play can feel useless in that we don't have anything tangible to show for it when we're done. But how can frivolous things actually be quite useful? What intangible things do they offer us?

3. What was the last thing you did just for the joy of it? How did you feel before? How did you feel after?

4. How can doing "useless" things help us tune in to the work of God in our spirits and in the world?

5. What is one enjoyable but non-essential thing you can do today? Will you?

6

Seek Adventure

Make voyages. Attempt them.
There's nothing else.
—TENNESSEE WILLIAMS

When I was eleven years old, my parents drove my sisters and me to a nearby state park to go rock climbing with Dad's friend, Don.[70] Don is a loud laugher and a rule-breaker, the kind of guy who once rigged up a dummy with a Bill Clinton mask in his passenger seat to avoid getting ticketed while driving alone in the carpool lane.

"Look!" he showed my sisters and me. "When I pull this string, Bill waves to the cops!"

Years earlier, Don had landed a tiny plane at our local, small-town airport not long after he'd gotten his pilot's license, offering us all a ride. I screamed for the entire four bone-chilling minutes of our flight together before my piercing shrieks forced him to land. (Later we saw him de-icing the wings with a credit card. *A credit card.*)

But even after that, my parents thought it would be a good idea to let Don take us all rock climbing, because apparently he knew a lot about knots and hadn't killed anyone yet.

He rigged up ropes, gave out harnesses, and spent the next few hours guiding us up the face of a forty-foot cliff. My sisters made it halfway. I made it up a little higher. Then Don, being Don, raised the stakes.

"Who wants to rappel?" he crowed. My sisters and I had had enough by now. We were more interested in sneaking forbidden sodas out of the cooler while the adults were distracted. Noticing his flagging audience, Don seized on my mom.

"Barb! Want to rappel?"

My mom is a pretty adventurous lady. Despite her suburban Chicago roots, she spent months of her childhood fishing at my grandparents' cabin in northern Wisconsin where she learned to bait a hook like the best of them. She once went whitewater rafting down the Colorado River while eight months pregnant with my sister Caitlyn. (Cait turned out to be the family daredevil. Go figure.) She's backpacked through the Canadian Rockies with girlfriends—a trip my dad was more than happy to pass on. He likes to quote Jim Gaffigan: "I'm *indoorsy*."

So Mom only hesitated a second before following Don up the trail that led to the top of the ridge. My dad, my sisters, and I waited at its base, trading fruit snacks, chomping on apples, and drawing in the dirt. After fifteen minutes, we were antsy. After half an hour, we were bored. After forty-five minutes, we were *over it*. My dad told us to stay put and headed up the trail to check on things.

We'd had two sodas apiece by the time we saw my mom beginning to descend the cliff. She stepped off slowly at first, inches of rope sliding through her hands, and then faster, whizzing down in a graceful arc before slowing to land softly in a small puff of dust.

"Where *were* you?" asked Caitlyn.

"What *took* so long?" I asked.

"We drank all the soda," admitted Caroline.

"CAROLINE!!!" Cait and I yelled.

"It took me a while to let go," said my mom. "Stepping backward off a cliff is pretty scary. It went against every instinct I have."

"Was it fun?" Cait asked.

"It was *so* fun," said my Mom, unclipping from the rope. "I'm going again."

The next time, Dad went, too.

Adventure can wake up the soul. Two Christmases ago, Lincoln (then seven years old) received the book *50 Dangerous*

Things You Should Let Your Children Do and immediately set himself the goal of doing them all. We began our festal Christian holiday with him asking us how many times we thought he could lick a nine-volt battery and ended it with him crying because we wouldn't let him jump off the roof.

"That would work if we had *snow*," Daryl and I protested. Frustrating moments aside, encouraging our kids to engage in a little healthy and age-appropriate danger is good for them and for us. Engaging in it ourselves is just as necessary.

Perhaps the best contemporary essay I've ever read is Annie Dillard's "Total Eclipse." (Brian Benson's "Central Heating" gives it a run for its money, and every single American ever needs to read Martin Luther King Jr's "Letter from a Birmingham Jail," but for pure breathtaking beauty, I think Dillard's still comes out on top.) I've never seen an eclipse, but her words, written after witnessing it with hundreds of others on a hillside outside Yakima, Washington in 1979, put me there.

> PLAYFULNESS INVITES US TO TAKE RISKS THAT WILL GET OUR HEARTS PUMPING WITH JOY.

> The second before the sun went out we saw a wall of dark shadow come speeding at us. We no sooner saw it than it was upon us, like thunder. It roared up the valley. It slammed our hill and knocked us out. It was the monstrous swift shadow cone of the moon. I have since read that this wave of shadow moves 1,800 miles an hour.

Language can give no sense of this sort of speed—1,800 miles an hour. It was 195 miles wide. No end was in sight—you saw only the edge. It rolled at you across the land at 1,800 miles an hour, hauling darkness like plague behind it. Seeing it, and knowing it was coming straight for you, was like feeling a slug of anesthetic shoot up your arm. If you think very fast, you may have time to think, "Soon it will hit my brain." You can feel the deadness race up your arm; you can feel the appalling, inhuman speed of your own blood. We saw the wall of shadow coming, and screamed before it hit.[71]

Rarely a week goes by when I don't think about Dillard on that hillside, screaming. That an eclipse should drive a Pulitzer-prize winning author to her most animalistic instincts so quickly chastens and intrigues me. Even knowing it was coming was no safeguard against its terror. Earlier in the essay Dillard muses that, had she *not* known the eclipse was expected, she would have "died of fright on the spot" like Emperor Louis of Bavaria. How easily we take light for granted until it vanishes.

The inverse of her terror occurs when the light returns, roaring down the valley in the same way and at the same speed the darkness first appeared. Calm is restored: albeit a new, introspective calm. A deeper happiness. She will never be the same.

We see this same change in countless figures within the pages of Scripture. God calls; they answer. The adventure begins. Abram is asked to leave his homeland behind—at the young, frisky age of seventy-five.[72] Moses is told to go back to the land of Egyptian oppression—a place he escaped by the skin of his teeth—to help free God's people from slavery. Esther is called to stand before a tyrannical king with a request that is likely to get her killed (but doesn't!). Paul is shipwrecked, imprisoned, and driven out of town by angry mobs. From Genesis to Revelation, God's leading will nearly always bring us out of our comfort zones. A life spent seeking God is always, always an adventure. Sometimes seeking that adventure is as simple as a prayer: "God, what do you have for me today? Help me to follow you with courage."

Haircuts and Happiness

Adventure isn't just freeing. It's *fun*, too. Even small adventures can put a spring in our step. For example: what would you wear if you didn't get dressed in the morning with an eye to what others would think? (I mean, you should probably wear *clothes*, don't get me wrong, but who's to say chartreuse is in and teal is out? You do you!) In *Uncluttered* I wrote of my all black-white-and-denim wardrobe, which was great for simplicity but bad for making it through a pandemic with good cheer. Now I basically dress like Ms. Frizzle from *The Magic School Bus*. Bring on the palm tree t-shirts. What activity excites you that you haven't tried because it's just too daunting? Impostor syndrome be darned: write that novel and then let someone else read it. Submit that application. Take that trapeze class. Ask that person you've admired from a distance if they'd like to go out for fro-yo. Sign up for the mission trip. Coach the team, whether or not you are a fan of orange slices. Teach the Sunday School class, especially if you're not an expert in all things Bible. (Teaching has a wonderful way of helping the teacher learn, too!) Wear the bright lipstick. Try the *hot*, hot sauce.

Back during my college years, I went to an upscale Chicago salon for my first real professional cut. I'd dabbled in small-town beauty parlors before, but nothing turned out very stylish, and I usually ended up trying to salvage it at home later with my mom's sewing scissors and a box of generic dye from the Pick n' Save grocery. When my hair started to turn yellow-orange because apparently you can't get the same results for seven dollars' worth of grocery store chemicals that you can from professional-grade hair dye, it was time for an intervention. I put on

> A LIFE SPENT SEEKING GOD IS ALWAYS, ALWAYS AN ADVENTURE.

my favorite/only trendy sweater and arrived at the salon's front counter breathless and excited. This was the big leagues.

I sipped apple juice in the chair as a heavily-tattooed fifty-something guy named Dirkson spread a cape over my shoulders with a bullfighter's flourish, spun me around, and tilted his head to the side, studying me from crown to chin.

"You have a lovely, oval-shaped face," he said. "A little round, but not too round." He bit his lip. "Nice eyes. Yes, nice eyes.

But—" and here he turned stern and held up a finger, "—you should never *ever* have bangs." I nodded. Dirkson clearly knew more about hair than I ever would. He must be right. There were simply no questions to be asked.

He gave me a cut I didn't love but received lots of compliments on and fixed my tropical fruit-colored hair by dying it a dark bay brown.

"This is your natural color," he told me. I nodded. It wasn't.

What I really took away from my time in Dirkson's chair was his word about bangs. That I should never have them. Never *ever*. Over the next decade, I sat in stylists' chairs around the country, too afraid to go against his proclaimed wisdom. What would happen if I defied him? Surely he knew best; he was a professional! All I knew about hair was that I grew it and was super bad at coloring it.

These little comments stick with us, don't they? The mean thing that girl said in elementary school. The offhanded remark from a neighbor. The words spoken flippantly by a family member. Mere opinion, spoken and received as Gospel truth. But we don't need to let those comments define us. There *is* truth, and it is holy and sacred and beautiful, but it simply does not extend to haircuts. Those are a matter of preference, and we are allowed to live as dangerously as we dare.

Friends, I'm getting *bangs*.

Silent Night Fright

Going to church on Christmas Eve smelled like hairspray. No one dresses up much in rural Wisconsin. Most folks spend seven days a week in jeans. Green Bay Packer hoodies are not uncommon at church on a Sunday morning. But on the Christmas Eves of my childhood, folks got fancy and fancied their kids up, too. And the whole thing smelled like Aqua Net.

My sisters and I scurried around the entryway looking for matching mittens and shoes while Dad warmed up the car.

"Mommmm!" Caitlyn yelled, holding up a half-eaten pair of Mary Janes.

"Bogey, *NO!*" my mom said, waving the shoe an inch from our chocolate Labrador's face. Bogey was essentially a canine floor rug that pooped and ate. He rarely moved from his spot in the living room, and the only remotely naughty thing he ever did—and he did it regularly—was chew up our patent leather dress shoes.

"You're just going to have to wear your boots," Mom said, causing Caitlyn to sigh in abject despair. Though she's the sportiest of us sisters by far, she also spent her school years caring *profoundly* about being cool. I always knew that target was too far away to reach. My inherent nerdiness was freeing, in a strange way.

"Fine," Mom said. "Uh... here. Try these." She pulled a pair of low pumps from the back of the closet.

"She gets to wear HIGH HEELS?!" Caroline said. "My shoes are chewed, too!" She pointed to a ratty toe.

"Everybody! Get in the car!" Mom commanded as Bogey quietly slipped the last unscathed Mary Jane over to the living room for a good gnawing.

"We're going to be late," Dad said as we slid the minivan door shut. Arriving five minutes early counts as late to my dad, which is why I'm neurotically early to everything to this day. He tuned the radio to Christmas carols, and we settled in for the twenty cold miles of evergreen forests between us and church, broken only by the occasional gas station and Weasel's Exotic Dancing, which we rarely passed without one or both of my parents reminding us that we were NEVER under ANY CIRCUMSTANCES to set foot on the property. (They were super thrilled years later when my friend Jessie and I ran out of gas on our way home from church and had to pull into that parking lot and wait for reinforcements. The only saving grace was that Weasels was definitely not open at noon on a Sunday.)

> "LAUGHTER IS THE CLOSEST THING TO THE GRACE OF GOD." –KARL BARTH

That Christmas Eve night, at the blackest stretch of road, our minivan hit a patch of glare ice, invisible and deadly. At sixty miles per hour, we flew out of control, Dad's efforts to pump the brakes powerless against such velocity.

"Hold on!" he screamed, and we screamed too, grabbing armrests, door handles, each other. The car spun a complete 360°, slamming us all into the sides of our seats, flinging a travel mug from its cup holder, loosening hair scrunchies, and shooting adrenaline through our bodies like fire.

And then, somehow, my dad wrestled control back again. We pointed forward. A hush fell over the car.

Dad blew the air out of his lungs and gently braked, pulling us to the edge of the road, a tight squeeze with the snowbank. We breathed in and out.

Then Caroline began to laugh.

"What *was* that?" she asked.

"That was *amazing!*" Caitlyn shouted. My parents looked at each other. Bing Crosby continued his crooning.

Ten minutes later, we pulled into the church parking lot and trudged in through the snow, still smiling.

Karl Barth is credited with saying that "laughter is the closest thing to the grace of God."[73] At the service's end, I looked down the pew, aware we should probably have ended up in the hospital or frostbitten or dead; but instead, this Christmas Eve would always be marked by that sacred space between the out-of-control-car and the continuation of our journey, when we paused to breathe together on the side of the frozen road in our chewed up shoes and Aqua-Netted hair. I watched the candle-glow in my younger sisters' eyes, in my parents', and we sang together.

All is calm. All is bright.

And it was. It was.

ACCEPT THE INVITATION
Seek Adventure

1. Read John 6:63–69. How is following Jesus an adventure?

2. Do you long for adventure or prefer safety and comfort? Why?

3. Has anyone ever told you that you shouldn't or couldn't do something, in a way that you've carried with you? Were they right, or can you lay down their words and consider a new adventure?

4. How does risk connect us to joy? What is one way you can seek adventure this week? This month? This year?

Invest in Community

*I have learned that the best way to lift
one's self up is to help someone else.*
—BOOKER T. WASHINGTON

W hen I was in seminary, up to my eyeballs in Hebrew language classes, working three jobs, and barely having time to feed myself, my friend Katie would come banging on my apartment door.

"Can I come in?" she'd yell.

"I'm studying!" I'd say.

"I don't care!" she'd say. "I made smoothies!"

Most of us have that friend—you know the one—with whom it is impossible to sustain a bad mood. They bring the jokes and the smiles, the hugs and the compassionate, listening ears; they're more closely related to Tigger than Eeyore. Or perhaps you *are* that friend, and if so, God bless you. Keep it up.

People help forge pathways to playfulness, reminding us of the big, wide, beautiful world outside our own mind. When our kids are in a grumpy funk, we've found that performing an act of kindness for someone else almost always helps to snap them out of it: whether that's baking cookies, sweeping a sidewalk, or writing a letter. It's far easier to remain unhappy alone, and much harder to sustain our own happiness on our own. One of the most crushing effects of COVID-19 was the self-isolation required. While young working parents like me were stressed to the max trying to manage our children's distance learning and our jobs, I wouldn't trade my houseful for the bone-crushing loneliness my single friends experienced. (Though my husband and I did occasionally fantasize about all the books we'd read if we weren't busy making macaroni and cheese with one hand and keeping the toddler out of the dishwasher with the other, all while counting beats for our older son's piano practice and pleading with our younger son to *please* stop taking every pillow off of every bed to make his nine hundredth fort. A week or so of isolation from our totally wonderful but OH MY WORD SO ENERGETIC children would have been quite okay with us.)

THE WONDERFUL THING ABOUT INVESTING IN PEOPLE IS THAT IT DOESN'T HAVE TO BE A HEAVY LIFT OR EVEN TAKE MUCH TIME.

"I just need a *hug*," one friend told me, after diligently following her state's stay-at-home orders for months.

"I just need to *see people*," said another. "In a non-virtual way."

Even small social interactions with strangers can have a significant positive impact on our mood. University of Chicago behavioral scientist Nicholas Epley conducted a series of experiments on bus and train commuters, discovering that even small, kind social gestures like eye contact, nods, and smiles increased the happiness of those he studied: "The mood boost of talking to strangers may seem fleeting, but the research on well-being, Epley says, suggests that a happy life is made up of a high frequency of positive events, and even small positive experiences make a difference."[74]

The wonderful thing about investing in people is that it doesn't have to be a heavy lift or even take much time. A kind word to a neighbor from the other end of the driveway, a "How's your day going?" to our mail carrier when she's filling our box, or a nod to that guy next to us in line at the grocery store can be enough for a little boost of happiness. Yet another reason to put our phone in our pocket for a moment or two and look up and around.

Friendsgiving

Living far from family means we sometimes celebrate holidays with just the five of us. Southern California, like many major metropolitan areas, is made up largely of transplanted people. Our neighbors are from Mexico and Iran, northern California and South Carolina. Our church has a few Orange County lifers, but many more from the East Coast and the Pacific Northwest and the Heartland, from Iran and Korea, Ukraine and Indonesia and South Africa. Our little family is not the only one making new traditions in a new place. Hungry for a full table and a bustling house (not to mention blissfully unaware that we were living in the "before times" of serious viral danger), we sent out *Friendsgiving* invites to those we knew to also be living far from home.

> PLAYFULNESS INVITES US TO POUR INTO OTHERS, BECAUSE PLAY— LIKE MOST THINGS— IS EVEN BETTER WHEN SHARED.

"I'm sure most of them will be traveling," I told Daryl. "We can send out a big invite, because lots of people won't be able to come."

Surprise, surprise, they were *all in town*. Of the forty-five we invited, we got forty-one yeses and one additional "can I bring so-and-so, too?" I looked at our dining room table, which seats eight, and our borrowed card table, which would seat four more, and began counting every chair in the house and the yard. Even if we included the piano bench and the camping chairs, we still fell far short.

Plus (I probably shouldn't admit this in writing, but here we go) the thing is, I don't like people that much. A person is just fine—I enjoy meeting for coffee or chatting on the phone or going for a walk one-on-one. But when gatherings grow past a certain number, my soul begins to seize up with terror. I'm an introvert's introvert, quickly drained by being with people. The more people present, the more I'm drained. Ditto with the duration of the gathering. I adore our family Christmases, but it also takes me well past New Year's to recover from the CONSTANT SOCIAL INTERACTION EVERY DAY EVEN BEFORE COFFEE OH MY GOSH.

I knew I'd found a kindred spirit in seminary when one professor asked our class why we'd chosen to go into ministry.

"I just really like people," said the man sitting in front of me.

"Oh, you do, do you?" asked the professor. "Have you met people?" Guy had a point.

"It'll be great," Daryl said of our planned Friendsgiving. "Let's think playfully."

I hate it when he uses my own writing projects against me.

After some prayer and discussion, we sent a follow up email turning Friendsgiving into a potluck. We borrowed chairs from the neighbors. I baked pies. We roasted so much tri-tip. The night of Friendsgiving, we gathered in our backyard (California is merciful to big gatherings that way) and circled up for a prayer of gratitude for the friends who'd chosen to celebrate with us. We feasted together, refilling drinks, savoring fruit salad, passing out slices of pie.

"The friends came to my house," our three-year-old proclaimed proudly. "To *my* house."

I thanked God for a husband who helped me push through my momentary panic—*so many people!*—and my desire for everything to be just so. You can host a particularly fancy dinner party for eight or ten people, but you probably have to let some of that fussiness go if you're welcoming four dozen. When the house is bursting at the seams, the living room rug can be a chair, too. Welcoming a crowd nudged me into playfulness, into delight. Just weeks earlier I would have fretted and panicked, but my eyes were beginning to open. Isn't this often how God meets us—with blessings we didn't know we needed, and encounters we didn't expect? And God so regularly uses other people to bring us joy.

The lessons of improv flow right into the lessons of community. In *Silence and Other Surprising Invitations of Advent*, Enuma Okoro unpacks this kind of providential disruption: "Life's arbitrariness and God's unpredictability are not one in the same. This is why spiritual discernment and faith within community is a necessary element of perceiving and receiving holy disruptions—the movements of God that interrupt our life plans but ultimately bring order to our lives."[75] Sit with that for just a moment. God's movements, that so often seem like interruptions to us, are what *ultimately bring us order*. Whoa. I so often behave as though I need to manage all the details and control every small piece; yet when I surrender to God's designs, the path is always a better one. God draws us to community, to growth, to rest, to solitude, and ultimately, always deeper into joy.

"This is the way," God says in Isaiah. "Walk in it."[76]

In worship the Sunday after Friendsgiving, Wilson jumped from my lap during the opening hymn to go sit with friends who'd dined at our table. They welcomed him with open arms and, I'd even say, delight.

The Church that Plays Together

When a community is stressed, playfulness becomes even more important. In the midst of tension, playfulness helps maintain connections between people and can foster creative solutions. On the other side of difficulties, it can bolster and enhance recovery, reconnection, and rebuilding efforts. Though we tend to feel least playful in stressful seasons, it's often then that we can benefit from playfulness the most.

A couple of years ago, my friend, the brilliant actor Sonia Justl Ellis (no relation), discovered that she had a particular gift for facilitating her congregation having fun. "We'd just moved to Texas from New York," she told me, "and I just noticed that our church was so down, and my heart was so heavy. And God just reminded me, 'Sonia, you put on plays. You do theater. You're an entertainer! Cheer this congregation up! That is what I want you to do right now.'" For a time she fought with God, arguing, "That's not a real ministry! I need to be at a soup kitchen and I need to be teaching Sunday School!" But God was persistent. (He always is, isn't he?)

Sonia continued: "I came up with the idea to do a church talent show. And [the congregation] laughed together and played games together, and our church had never done anything just fun like this. And then I thought, we need to do a fall festival! And we did! I took on this role of 'church fun coordinator.'" As she organized playful opportunities within her congregation, Sonia saw doors open to greater collaboration, connection, and joy. Sometimes she set up a big event, but after a couple of these, as the church's collective mood began to lift and open, play bubbled up in all sorts of places. A big event can be a great trigger for change, but smaller avenues of play— gathering around donuts after worship, adding a joke or two into a sermon, involving children and their delightful messes and noise in fellowship gatherings—are remarkably effective as well.

Even with these initial successes, Sonia faced the nagging voice of doubt that her ministry wasn't *real* or *spiritual* enough. Then, as she saw its positive effects over time, she began to realize it was just as important as any other ministry of the church, as it completely reenergized the church's health, fellowship, and mission.

"I realize now I was doing something that added to our spiritual life," she said. "This wasn't just fluff; it *was* spiritual and was good for our growth and our bonding."[77]

Sometimes a pastor can be the one to help set the tone for a more playful, innovative, engaged church. Our congregation was eager to hear from Jackson, our senior pastor, on his first Sunday back from sabbatical. Many felt that his decision to spend time at a Benedictine monastery in Italy was an odd choice for a Presbyterian; he didn't even speak Italian. Everyone missed him.

As he gave the opening welcome, he expressed his gratitude for the time away and his excitement to be back. "You know," he said, "if I was really practicing Benedictine hospitality this morning with all of you, I'd have washed your hands on the way in, as a sign of welcome." The congregation stirred. This seemed tender and sweet, albeit a little bit strange. Had our relaxed, kind, mountain-biking pastor come back from Europe irreversibly altered?

"I would have done that," he said, "except..." We waited for what he'd say next. What was the holy reason he chose not to? Was it a Protestant/Catholic divide? A logistical conundrum? Something that would happen, instead, later in the service?

"I would have done it, except that would have been *a lot of work.*" And there it was. People chuckled. He grinned. Jackson was back, and any fears that he'd returned untouchably holy dissipated in the steamy California air. As he shared more about how he encountered God in daily prayer and regular Scripture study, we were ready now to listen and hear.

Churches that play together regularly develop bonds of friendship and fellowship that help sustain them during times of conflict or difficulty. Playfulness boosts resilience, too, and can help worshiping bodies bounce back more quickly as well as think through problems in innovative ways. When Paul first described the church as a body with "many members," all contributing something unique and helpful to the organism as a whole, he probably didn't have a church softball league in mind. But I'm guessing if there'd been one available, he'd have been first at bat.

Block Parties

Statistics on America's lack of regular interactions with our neighbors are staggering. Just over half of Americans know *some* of their neighbors, while only a quarter know *most* of them. Social events among neighbors are relatively rare, and it makes no difference whether people in a neighborhood have children or not.[78] What a far cry from the average neighborhood half a century ago, when children regularly played together outdoors. Many of my friends in their sixties or seventies remember games of kick-the-can that lasted until the streetlights blinked on at dusk. Today, the majority of our neighbors only allow their children to play out front if they—the parents—are standing right there. One told me she fears kidnappers. Of course, safety is important, and children are precious. A small child shouldn't be left alone to toddle into traffic. A preteen should have that helmet squarely on his noggin while out on his bike. But here's the thing: my family lives in *literally* the safest city of our size *in America*.

Yet still, the majority of parents I talk to lead with the worry that, if they let their kids out front to play, something terrible will happen. Fear—even unwarranted fear—can hamstring a community.

One way to push through this fear is by building relationships. When we first moved to our new neighborhood, I was hesitant to let Lincoln—then just five years old—play in our unfenced front yard alone. Daryl disagreed, but I was firm in my resolve.

"He's *five years old,*" I said. "*Anything could happen.*" Yet over the days that followed, we met the neighbors right across the street. They had six children and played out front nearly every day. Occasionally their older girls would babysit for us. Farther down the cul-de-sac, we met neighbors who had been on the street for two or even three decades. A junior high boy taught Lincoln to shoot hoops. A preteen girl challenged him to a game of tic-tac-toe with sidewalk chalk. Suddenly my fears began to dissipate. The unknown can be terrifying; but as we developed relationships with our neighbors, I discovered a community of kind, quirky, thoughtful people who believed that old adage that it takes a village to raise children. Suddenly, letting Lincoln play out front without us didn't mean that he was alone. He rode bikes with David and Peter, bounced a basketball with Aubrey and Elizabeth, and pulled a wagon full of the littlest kids from the block—Lillian and Mary, Caroline and Olivia, Braxton and Kayden.

Worry breaks down when it encounters a supply of positive information. It's one more reason investing in people helps us become more playful and free. A year later, when I went into labor with baby Felicity a few days earlier than expected, we didn't need to drive across town to a church friend's home. We simply walked Wilson across the street to our neighborhood family.

"It's time," Daryl said. Their kids started jumping up and down.

"Baby day?" they asked. Wilson headed into the herd of children with a huge smile and didn't look back.

A couple summers ago, these neighbors asked if we'd like to throw a block party.

"Yes," I said, and then immediately began qualifying my answer. "Except I don't really know how to do that. I've never even *been* to one before. I grew up in a forest."

Terri laughed and assured me that it would be easy.

"I'll make the invitations," she said. "The only other things we need are hot dogs and drinks. The neighbors will do the rest." This simple phrase began to set my heart at ease. Fellowship isn't something we *do* for others; it's something we do *with* them. I wasn't sure how to run a block party, but I could certainly manage hot dogs and buns if I didn't need to play Grand Hostess as well. With the date set, kids from the cul-de-sac started dropping by to ask questions.

"Can I bring my bike?" asked one.

"Will there be water balloons?" asked another. The day of the party, a preteen from the end of the street knocked on our door.

"How can I help?" she asked. We hauled out folding tables and chairs, plastic tablecloths and board games, and put E-Z ups overhead for shade. John, our next-door neighbor, hauled out a big speaker, and we hooked it up to a playlist featuring the Beach Boys and Johnny Cash. Neighbors emerged from their houses with potato salad and Popsicles, a birthday cake for a kid turning fourteen, watermelon cut up into triangles. When we needed more shade, Jeff and Dawn found another E-Z up in their garage. When the kids got hyper, Cooper brought out a football. Neighbors who'd lived on the street for decades began sharing stories about the block parties they'd thrown in years past, with kids now grown and moved away. After a few drinks, the tales turned even more exciting. *Did you know that the abandoned house is filled with bees? That your house's previous owner owned a whole pack of dogs? That the guy who lives over there is a nudist?*

> WORRY BREAKS DOWN WHEN IT ENCOUNTERS A SUPPLY OF POSITIVE INFORMATION.

We'd scheduled the party from 4–7 pm, but 7:00 came and went and things were still hopping. Someone gave the kids glow sticks, and as the sun settled down behind the eaves of the houses on the eastern side of the street, children spun around on bikes and trikes, whooping and hollering, leaving flashes of color in their wakes. We put the baby to bed and went back outside to play. After going inside a second time an hour later to put the older boys to bed, we returned to the street to discover that our neighbors had cleaned up everything without us.

In the days that followed, we watched a new ease and closeness descend on our street. People had always stopped to chat— ours is a rare southern California community of folks who have stayed put for more than a handful of years—but now they lingered, sharing worries about upcoming surgeries and hopes about job interviews, joining each other's elation at surprising joys and victories.

Investing in people—whether one-on-one or in big groups, digitally or in person—is one of the surest paths to happiness. For me, a quiet dinner with a friend or two often offers the biggest boost; but then, I'm an introvert. Extroverts flock to the block parties that give them the energy infusion they need. But that doesn't mean those of us with quieter souls can't benefit from a group gathering, and vice versa. There is, as the writer of Ecclesiastes reminds, "a time for everything."

Plus, it turns out you don't need much to plan a block party. Invite some friends, call out the neighbors, turn on some 80s tunes, and rummage in the freezer for Popsicles. It doesn't have to be complicated. The extroverts always show up. (Bless them.)

And if you're anything like little ol' introverted me, you'll find yourself surprised more often than not by the joy that comes from just being with people, with no agenda in mind. We had so much fun that we planned another one two months later.

And I don't mean to brag, but those hot dogs were *lit*.

ACCEPT THE INVITATION
Invest in Community

1. Read Acts 2:42–47. What can we learn from the way people in the early church invested in one another? What parallels do you see in your own friendships today? What differences do you note?

2. One of the studies shared in this chapter talks about the simple joy of a mundane social interaction, like nodding to someone you pass on the street. Where do you most often have these types of interactions in your life? How can you be on the lookout for these small happiness boosts?

3. What's the last thing your church did just for fun? Does Sonia Ellis' "fun ministry" appeal to you? Why or why not? How might God be calling you to bless your church with the gift of fun?

4. Have you ever been part of a neighborhood party? What was it like? Who could you join forces with to throw a neighborhood party in the coming months?

8

Play Small

Do you suppose, that part of the constant delight of Heaven, will be the ability to be truly thankful for everything, no matter how miniscule?
—MEREDITH ALLADY

"Well, this is embarrassing," I said, tallying my latest Scrabble move on the wall-hanging board in the church office. Our worship director, Jeff, was beating me by nearly a hundred points.

"Oh, did you take your turn?" Our youth director, Matt, came out of his office and picked up his rack of letter tiles. He scanned the board. "Perfect," he said. "You didn't take the spot I wanted." He carefully lined up all of his tiles and grinned. "Triple word score," he said, "*and* a Bingo." I gaped. Scrabble-aficionados know well that using all seven letters in a single turn means you receive an *additional* fifty points.

"But that means ..."

"I'm now beating you by more than two hundred points, yes. Don't you have a master's degree in English?"

"I don't really want to talk about that right now."

In the few months since Matt brought in Scrabble, I'd yet to win a game, despite my memorizing all of the two-letter-words. Still, we'd all upped our smack-talk, and nothing helped my sermons like a ten-minute break in front of the Scrabble board.

Playfulness doesn't have to be a big investment in time or resources to make a difference. Just a few moments—or even a few seconds!—can spark the release of stress and influx of creativity we need.

In my interview with play therapist Malaika Clelland, she emphasized the ease and importance of micro-play. "Play in general is just reflecting rather than directing," she told me. "I tell parents, 'Don't ask questions and don't teach.' The funny thing is, when I watch a parent and child play, that's often the first two things a parent goes to."

"I'm *totally* guilty of that," I said. "Wilson just wants to build a fort, and I'm trying to get him to count the pillows so we can turn it into an enrichment activity. Also, fort-building gets really old for me really fast." She laughed.

"Oh yeah, it is *not* easy," she said. "I remember trying to play My Little Pony toys with my daughters and just feeling like, 'This is *so* boring.'"

"Or I subtly try to do a chore during playtime," I said. "Wilson will be in his fort and I'll be halfway in the fort but also folding laundry to the side."

"Right! Because there's a lot to do!"

"Exactly. And if I play with him for an hour, the laundry's still undone. But he totally notices when I've mentally checked out, and he *hates* it." I paused and took a breath, deciding whether or not to admit the depth of my play struggles to an expert in the field. "But even more than that," I said, "I think I really struggle to play because it feels so unproductive. My lists are long, my house is messy, and my email box is full. Yet what you're telling me is that playing is one of the best things I can do with my kids because of the connection it builds."

> PLAYFULNESS INVITES US TO ENGAGE IN SHORT-TERM FUN AND BE ON THE LOOKOUT FOR SIMPLE PLEASURES.

"Just get on the floor," she said. "Connecting with your kids ten minutes a day can make a huge difference. With kids, our job is to really be witnesses, and just be there with them."

"Ten minutes a day?" I asked. "Wow. I might be able to do that."

"You totally can," she said. "Anyone can."

Intrigued by the invitation to start small, I began seeking to give myself playful permission in my everyday life: at church, at home, with my children, while driving. Perhaps it *didn't* need to be that complicated. If I didn't have hours to give, I could play where I was, with what I had, at any moment. I could play for ten seconds, or even five. Play researcher Lawrence J. Cohen agrees with Malaika that it's okay to start really small, especially when playing with kids. "Make funny faces," he writes. "Fall down a lot."[79]

My friend April is a master of this type of play. She leads music classes for young children and their caregivers, teaching parents and grandparents and nannies to play musically with their children both inside and outside of class.

RETRAINING OURSELVES IN PLAY CAN BE AS SIMPLE AS HUMMING A TUNE IN THE SHOWER OR TURNING ON SOME MUSIC WHILE WE WASH DISHES.

With April's guidance, Lincoln fell in love with drumming (we are not sure yet whether or not to thank her for this), Felicity learned to keep a rhythm before she could speak, and our entire family occasionally breaks into renditions of "The Old Brass Wagon" (or, as Wilson calls it, "The Old Gas Wagon"). I've seen her persuade dignified older men to dance with rainbow-colored scarves and even the most stubborn toddlers crack a smile when she brings out the shaker eggs. April encourages us to practice musical micro-play, especially during times of transition.

When Wilson won't put his shoes on, I try to think of April and burst into silly songs. Bingo. Shoes on. When Lincoln wakes up under a black cloud, I let him choose a favorite tune and watch his brow slowly unfurrow with the beat. April's wisdom has even made our marriage more playful, with Daryl occasionally serenading me in the early morning hours with original, off-key compositions like "That Was a Gross Poopy Diaper," and "Darling, We Are Out of Ham."

"But I'm not musical," you might be protesting. "I can't carry a tune in a bucket, so how can I play musically?" Therein lies the rub. The only time I've ever seen April truly stern was when Daryl told her he couldn't sing.

"*Everyone can sing*," she said. "Whoever told you that was wrong. If you can talk, you can sing. And don't let your kids hear you say that—it's how people start losing the gift of music." Both chastened and heartened, Daryl has been singing ever since. And do you know what? He *can!*

Retraining ourselves in play can be as simple as humming a tune in the shower or turning on some music while we wash dishes. It's near-impossible to stay grouchy while whistling. Really! Try it! And if music isn't your thing, other ways to micro-play abound. Anything outdoors leaves lots of room for exploration and fun. Sports are obvious arenas for play, and not just organized team sports but picking up a ball to toss around for a few minutes. One college minister I know carries a Frisbee because students can't help but try to catch it when he tosses it their way. After the first toss, the game is on, and so is the connection.

Even chores can be an opportunity for play. Try turning putting the laundry away into a race, sweeping the floor into a game, cooking dinner into an episode of *Chopped*. Enjoyable work ceases to be work at all, and it's all the better if you can involve a friend as a teammate. Twitter is one of my favorite places to microplay, with witty banter among virtual friends often causing me to laugh out loud.

Daryl: What's so funny?

Me: Weird Christian Twitter. Homeschool memes. @TheCatWhisprer.

Daryl: I don't know what any of that means.

Play can also fill the gaps where anxiety, fear, or worry might otherwise overtake us. A woman at the first church I pastored told me that during a cancer scare she struggled to sleep.

"I'd lie awake all night worrying," she said. "So I decided, if I had time to worry, I had time to pray." I've thought of her words during many a sleepless night of my own. There is never any shortage of things to worry about. Her wisdom applies to play as well. If I have energy to fret, I have energy to play, and often when I open myself up to playfulness, solutions to the very thing I'd been worrying about begin to rise to the surface. These little teaspoons of new energy and joy can add up quickly. They can also make the day run a bit smoother— adding yet another drop to our bucket of happiness.

Playful Shortcuts

"A little help here?" I yelled to my husband as I tried to finagle my squirming, squalling preschooler into his car seat. Sweat trickled down my back, pooling at the waistband of my skirt.

"Noooooo!" three-year-old Wilson continued to yell. "Noooooo! I get down! I get out myself! Me! *ME*!"

As I wedged Wilson's arms through the straps, I leaned my face in, inches from his.

"You *have* to get buckled," I hissed. "We are running late for church. You cannot always do things yourself. Stop. Screaming." He fell silent, stilled for a nanosecond, then carried on thrashing.

While our firstborn thinned out like a string bean in his toddler years, our second, Wilson, is solid as a fire hydrant and strong as a baby ox. Sometimes I can barely contain him. He jutted out his little chin, pulled his arms back out of their straps, and glared at me, the Doer of All Bad Things, Forcer of Preschoolers into Car Seats, and Insister of Vegetables.

"Noooooooooooo!" he wailed. "ME DO IT!!!"

My husband Daryl tapped my shoulder.

"Tag out?" he asked.

"Gladly."

"Hey bud," he said, leaning over to tousle Wilson's blonde curls. "How fast can you get your arms into their straps?"

Wilson broke into a grin. He was fastened in by the time I made it to the passenger's side door.

"You've gotta *play* with him," Daryl said as we backed out of the driveway. Though Daryl has a PhD in Big Important Theological Things™, he is also almost always quicker to access his silly side, a quality I both envy and admire.

"We're running too late for play," I said.

"My way was faster," he noted with a half-smile. "And easier."

The playful way nearly always is.

Simple Pleasures

Because I grew up in the northwoods of Wisconsin and my husband grew up in the suburbs of Los Angeles, when we play the game "Who Was Cooler in High School," he wins by about eighteen thousand miles. He was a multi-sport athlete; I rode the soccer bench and then, later, the ice hockey one. He led his youth group; I ate lunch alone in the creative writing room. Then there were our school trips. As a high school senior in southern California, his entire graduating class got the run of Disneyland, exploring the park late into the night after it had closed to the public. This was in addition to trips to Magic Mountain, Knott's Berry Farm, the local symphony, and

Nickelodeon Studios. My graduating class, on the other hand, took the same field trip we'd taken the previous three years ... to the local cranberry bog.

If you've ever seen an Ocean Spray commercial, you have a basic idea of what a cranberry bog looks like. Cranberries are harvested in flooded trenches, floating to the surface on long stalks, where they bob serenely, round and red, awaiting the machines that will snip them off and carry them away once they reach peak ripeness. It's all very idyllic, but there's not much to *see*. Plus, what the commercials *don't* show is that temperatures are usually in the mid-30s, and sleet and freezing rain are common.

We'd pull up to these bogs in our yellow school buses and unload for the tour, our feet soon muddy, our fingers quickly freezing. We'd stamp and blow to try to stay warm, like a herd of acne-ridden ponies, while our guide explained how cranberries grow and the importance of their production to the economy of our fair state. Then we'd get back on the bus and eat lunch. Disneyland, it was not.

I've had a chip on my shoulder for years about the cranberry bog trips, not just because they were pretty dour but because there were actually other things we could have seen. Our state has a symphony, too, after all, and those bogs were *cold*.

I was mid-cranberry-bog-rant in front of Daryl and my youngest sister, Caroline, recently, when she stopped me cold.

"You didn't *like* visiting the cranberry bogs?" she asked.

"Not *four times*," I said. "That seemed a little excessive."

"Hm," she said. "You must have had a really different experience than I did. Did you get to go there on a school bus?"

"Yep."

"But wasn't that fun? I mean, to go somewhere other than school on a school bus?" I stared at her blankly.

"I guess … ?"

"And we got to see how the berries actually grow!" she continued. "They float! Isn't that cool?" Daryl began to chuckle.

"Seems it's all in how you look at it," he said.

"I loved that trip," Caroline said. "I looked forward to it every year."

Playfulness, like so many other things in life, is what you make of it. The smallest thing can bring joy if we are ready to receive it. "Listen to the birds," writes Richard Foster; "they are messengers of God."[80] There can be magic even in a soggy, muddy, chilly cranberry bog. Who knew?

The more I leaned into playing small, the more I realized that Caroline was right. Those trips had been a sort of delight. It just took me a couple of decades to see it.

Playing small is so simple. Toss a ball to the dog, check out a library book, run your fingers over a silky scarf or a nubby sweater. Be witty on Twitter, but then go outside. Turn the chore into a game. Turn up the music. Turn off the phone. Experiment in the kitchen. Take ten minutes and give yourself fully to whatever game a child wants to play. Sit down at the piano. Count the number of red cars you pass. Phone a friend. Use the fancy teacup. Play some jazz.

We sing a lot at our house these days, and though none of us will be auditioning for the opera anytime soon, it is helping us access a whole lot of micro-play. Perhaps music could be your way in, too. Try a jazzy rendition of "Darling, We Are Out of Ham" to get you started.

Trust me: it's a good one.

ACCEPT THE INVITATION
Play Small

1. Read Proverbs 30:24–28. What does the author say about the power of small things? How is each example a playful one?

2. Which example of micro-play appealed to you most, and why? How can you incorporate this into your life today—or even right now?

3. What is one simple pleasure in your life that you may have overlooked? How might you receive that simple pleasure for what it is, appreciating the joy it has to offer?

4. Scripture talks about moving mountains, but it also talks about the tiniest things—a mustard seed, a pearl, a sparrow, each hair on our heads. What significance do small things have to Jesus?

5. If you have children, when might you be able to give them ten minutes of pure, uninterrupted play today? If you don't have children, who in your life—perhaps a person, perhaps a pet—can you gift with ten minutes of playtime?

9

Fail Regularly

Failure is an option here. If things are not failing,
you are not innovating enough.
—ELON MUSK

Watching a spider on the shower ceiling and contemplating how, when it falls on my head, I'll begin flailing and screaming, slip, fall, and concuss myself (resulting in a brain aneurysm and death) is probably my least favorite hobby. Which reminds me: sometimes thinking through the worst-case scenario is actually a helpful tool in the pursuit of playfulness. Whether it's getting up in front of a room filled with people to try improv, signing up for that community education course even though you know absolutely *nothing* about horticulture, or picking up a paintbrush even though you're no Michelangelo, often your biggest fears will sound silly when you actually speak them aloud.

Daryl and I played this horrible-but-helpful game with Pastor Jackson before he left for a three-month sabbatical.

"What if a staff member dies?" I asked.

"What if there's a fire and we have to evacuate?" asked Daryl.

"What if *two* staff members die?" I asked.

"What if one of the youth group kids gets hurt up at camp?" asked Daryl.

"What if *three* staff members—"

"Court," said Daryl, "*seriously.*"

As we played out each of our doomsday scenarios, Jackson walked us through what he would do in that particular situation, who he'd call for support, which committees or elders or staff people to loop in so we wouldn't be alone. "I'd call Carol," he said, naming our lead office administrator. "I'd call the Finance elder." "I'd call Forrest at the Presbytery offices." "I'd call the parents first, then the youth leaders, then the camp." In the last couple of weeks before we'd be taking the reins, saying goodbye to our fearless leader as he headed off for some much-needed rest and prayer, he gave us a great gift. We sent him away feeling confident and equipped. And despite my worst fears, not a single staff person died.

PLAYFULNESS INVITES US TO LET GO OF PERFECTION IN ORDER TO INNOVATE, CREATE, AND TRY NEW THINGS, REMEMBERING THAT FAILURE IS RARELY FATAL.

We bumbled a bit; of course we did. But Jackson's kindness in releasing us to do our best freed us from the terror of what might happen if we made even a single misstep. Failure wasn't the enemy; paralysis was. And indeed, *fear* is often the greatest obstacle in our pursuit of playfulness. If we aren't free to fail, to look silly, to mess up and try again, we'll never be freed to play.

So ask yourself: what's the worst thing that could happen? You might not be good at volleyball! So what? You could try out for that community theater's production of *Cats* and not be cast. And? (I mean, really, that might be a blessing.) You could discover that you can't sauté a sea bass on *Master Chef*. People will forget about it in fifteen minutes. Or your senior pastor might go on sabbatical and you might surprise yourself by not accidentally burning the church to the ground. Though, as Jackson told us before he left, "Don't worry; we have insurance for that." Bless.

Perhaps we find such exhilaration in letting go because joy is our native country, where we feel at home at long last. When we begin to realize we don't have to be perfect; when we can start to chuckle at our own foibles and weaknesses; when we let go of control and fear, beautiful things can happen. Failure is not only okay, it's *necessary*. Important. Even, I'd argue, *essential*.

We're bad at failing, though. We prefer to succeed. Of course we do. Who doesn't? We'd rather focus on achievement, glory, and winning. We've championed the strong and successful so much we've forgotten that we serve a God who promises his power is "made perfect in weakness."[81] Failure has lessons to teach that nothing else can: lessons of faith, of learning, of creativity, and yes, even lessons of joy. When we realize that failure isn't fatal, we begin to truly live.

The freedom to fail allows us to hold ourselves tenderly, admitting our missteps, asking for help, learning and growing, and starting again. There is abundant grace in realizing we don't need to be perfect—that often those who love us dearest and best do it with all our faults fully in sight. Plus, the more we get to know Jesus, who he is and who we are in him, the greater our understanding that the work is the Lord's and we are simply sheep in his pastures. As Flannery O'Connor once wrote, "To know oneself is, above all, to know what one lacks... The first product of self-knowledge is humility."[82]

Lessons in Failure

Smith College recently began offering a course called "Failing Well," noting that failure is "not a bug of learning, it's the *feature*." Notes Bill Taylor in the *Harvard Business Review*:

> Indeed, when students enroll in [the] program, they receive a Certificate of Failure that declares they are "hereby authorized to screw up, bomb, or fail" at a relationship, a project, a test, or any other initiative that seems hugely important and "still be a totally worthy, utterly excellent human being." Students who are prepared to handle failure are less fragile and more daring than those who expect perfection and flawless performance.[83]

The expectation that failure won't end us, that instead it's a bridge to learning and growth, is a hallmark of tremendously successful people, institutions, and companies like Apple, Google, and Netflix. My own church's organizational health improved when we decided to take a flier on some new programs, let a few floundering things run their natural course, and celebrate both successes and failures with an eye to learning. We now debrief after events with the expectation that we'll have learned from both the ups and the downs, and that the downs aren't disastrous but instead, instructive. As James

THERE IS ABUNDANT GRACE IN REALIZING WE DON'T NEED TO BE PERFECT.

Joyce is thought to have observed, "Mistakes are the portals of discovery." Modeling a freedom to fail from the top has set our whole congregation at ease. Perfection isn't the goal; walking with Jesus is. And walking with Jesus is an inherently creative, courageous, and playful act.

A few months after I got married, I visited my friend Inga in the suburbs of Chicago. She had a work meeting, so I headed out on a walk around her winding, tree-lined neighborhood, drinking in the fall colors and rustling leaves and promptly forgetting that I tend to get lost in my own neighborhood, much less an unfamiliar one. As darkness fell, I was hopelessly discombobulated. The temperature plummeted, and I mentally berated myself for not grabbing a jacket. (It was Chicago, duh. *Always grab a jacket.*) GPS technology was still fairly new, and my cell phone didn't have it. So I called Inga—no answer. Then I called Daryl.

"What street are you standing on?" he asked. Then, "Walk to the nearest cross street and tell me what it says." I could hear him typing on his keyboard in the background. "Yep! Got it! All you have to do is keep walking and turn left."

"No," I told him. "I've tried that. Her house isn't that way." There was a long pause. Daryl had learned quite a bit about me in three months of marriage, including that I am at my most absolute pig-headedly stubborn when I don't actually know what I'm talking about.

"Welllll," he said, "then why don't you turn right instead."

"That sounds good," I said. We continued to chat as I walked, and after nearly a mile, I arrived on my friend's doorstep.

"Thank you *so* much," I told him. "You really saved me. I am freezing." Another long pause. A sigh.

"Court," he said. "You know I love you. But you could have been indoors fifteen minutes earlier if you'd turned left when I told you to."

"But the right turn got me home!" I protested.

"It did," he said. "But I had to reroute you blocks and blocks out of your way just because you—the lost person—decided you knew better."

"But—"

"Court," he said, not unkindly, "you called me for help. And I have the map."

Who questions the guy with the map, especially when they're freezing cold and desperate for help? Me. I do. A few nights later I expressed this shame to Daryl, who laughed.

"You are stubborn *beyond*," he said. "Especially when you're wrong. But I love you for it." My embarrassment slowly began to lift.

"You do?" I asked.

"Of course!" he said. "It's one of the things that makes you *you*. I mean, it'd make your life a little easier to *not* be so stubborn sometimes, but we are all a work in progress."

How absolutely lovely to be adored as a work in progress! Being a work in progress means that failure is part of the package. We will mess up. We will fall short. We will need to apologize, to confess, to repent, to get up and try again. But even in the midst of all of these shortcomings, we are loved deeply and profoundly by the God who created us, and by so many of the friends and family who walk alongside us. And in his patient rerouting, Daryl offered the grace for me to fail and still find myself safe.

> BEING A WORK IN PROGRESS MEANS THAT FAILURE IS PART OF THE PACKAGE.

How Delightful?

I heard an interview with a pop star once where the singer admitted that he's so introverted he often comes across as angry when fans ask him for a picture or an autograph.

"That's super off-putting for your fans," his wife told him. "What if, when someone came up to you like that, you thought in your head, 'How delightful!'"

It worked for him. I wondered if it could work for me—if, when faced with the standard difficulties of a day, the unpredictability of life with three children, the absolute grindy-ness of the daily grind, I could begin to gently nudge myself farther into the land of delight. Poet Ross Gay talks of personifying prickly emotions: even personifying the particular feeling of irritation as a "little annoyance monster who, for the record, never smiles and always wears a crooked bow tie." Sometimes, he notes, it's good to "poke a finger in its ribs."[84]

My first test arrived only a couple days later. For my last Sunday on maternity leave with our baby girl, we'd arranged to worship with friends up at their church in Pasadena, where for one delightful Sunday we'd be not pastors but just people, sitting in the pews with our brood, singing to Jesus, listening to a sermon we didn't prepare, delightfully anonymous.

Before the drive, Daryl and I each took a turn handing off the kids so we could get ready. I went first while he shoveled oatmeal and blueberries into the boys. While he showered, I gathered all of the supplies we'd need to take a kindergartener, a toddler, a newborn, an always-hungry dad, and a nursing mom with serious dietary restrictions sixty miles north. I packed diapers, baby wipes, bibs, water bottles, snacks, more snacks, even more snacks, baby blankets, burp cloths, picture books, pacifiers, rattles, the baby carrier that Daryl wears (it hurts my back), the baby carrier that I wear (it hurts *his* back), phones, wallets, keys. I shoved it all in the car and wrangled both of the boys into church clothes, surveying my handiwork with a small mountain's worth of pride. I'd *done* it! We were ready on time. It was a miracle, and I couldn't wait to see our friends, worship as a family, and chat with Daryl on the drive north. Shalom.

Of course it wouldn't be that easy.

To make it to church on time, we needed to leave by 9:30 a.m. At 9:25, toweling off in the bathroom, Daryl threw out an idea.

"It'd be fun to stay for lunch, too," he said, holding up his phone. "I found this Chinese restaurant with great reviews just a mile from the church, and it turns out Chris and Stephanie have time to hang out a bit. Sound okay?" Record scratch.

When we'd put this excursion on the calendar weeks earlier, our friends couldn't make lunch, so we decided to drive up to worship, after which our littles would nap in the car. Apparently Chris and Stephanie's availability had changed at the last minute, and Daryl, King of the Last-Minute-Fun-

Time, jumped on it, overjoyed—pushing his wife, Queen of the Planning Peoples, to the verge of a panic attack.

"Sound good?" he asked again, as my eyes welled with tears. Staying for lunch would likely involve napping the kids at our friends' home, which involved packing up twenty-six additional baby-and-kid items in the next five minutes. Staying meant I wouldn't get the nap I so desperately needed. Not to mention that if I'd known we were staying longer, I wouldn't have worn the Spanx I can endure for a maximum of four hours without becoming seriously Spangry.

"I … can't …" I began. Then I realized, this was my chance. I could be FUN. I could be SPONTANEOUS. *I COULD BE HAPPY.* Couldn't I? "Sounds good," I whispered, turning away so he wouldn't see my tears.

I loaded the kids into the car as Daryl threw a portable crib into the trunk. I ran back into the house for the baby's swaddle blanket and the toddler's love object, an extra outfit for the baby, another handful of diapers, and a stroller. I took lots of deep breaths and grimly tried to find my fun. *How delightful,* I muttered under my breath. *How delightful. How delightful. How utterly freaking delightful.*

As we began the drive, I prayed, "Lord, help me to hold this day with open hands. Help me to hang loose." The glaring sun beat down, giving me an instant headache. In the rush to load the car in five minutes with half of what we owned, I'd left my sunglasses on the kitchen table. "Lord, help me not to kill Daryl."

Only a few miles later, we found our way into an argument, his desire for freedom at odds with my need to be properly prepared. My mascara ran. He fumed. I sulked.

Then we slowly untangled our knotty attitudes, working to find one another again. It turned out he'd been feeling really cooped up over the past few weeks, his whole world shrunk down to just church and home. He was hungry to connect with friends. He didn't even know that Spanx were a thing. I shared with him how difficult it was for me to travel with a newborn and how I always did better with a little prep time. I told him how physically drained I was—more than with the first two babies, since now I was constantly chasing after two olders while still in recovery from birthing their sister—and how staying longer meant that I would miss out on the nap I desperately needed.

He reached for my hand. I gave it. It wasn't the easy drive I'd hoped for, but it was a deeper kind of delight. One worth working for.

I'd be lying if I told you all our family play attempts were successful, that Daryl and I no longer ever snap at each other or the kids, that we've mastered rest and playfulness and all their inherent delights. We haven't. But failure is rarely fatal. We get up, dust ourselves off, and try again. And we did.

Because here's the thing: play isn't just about *willing* yourself into the play style of someone else, even if you happen to love that someone a particularly large amount. It's also about being able to sit with yourself, wondering and noticing what brings you actual, easy joy. While nudging ourselves to try new things and perhaps even be a skosh more flexible can be a road to deeper happiness, playfulness also comes when we do the hard work of honesty with those we love.

The next time Daryl threw a spontaneous curveball into my perfectly planned day, I told him I wasn't willing to catch it, and he understood. The time after that, I held out my hands, taking one step closer to him in the dance of a playful marriage, as we both continued to learn how we played best, and how we could love each other in and across our vast gulf of differences.

As I mused about my own play-style, I arrived at the week of our planned summer staycation. Amidst beach days and backyard fort-building and family togetherness, Daryl and I agreed to gift each other twenty-four kid-free hours. No household responsibilities or pastoral work allowed. In fact, we'd go stay at a friend's empty house to ensure we couldn't even be tapped to unload the dishwasher, read a bedtime story, or kill a spider. After months of parenting and pastoring in a pandemic, twenty-four solid hours by myself sounded like the elixir of life. I was relatively certain I'd sleep for twenty-three of them, but just in case I didn't,

I pondered what I might like to do. What would actually be *effortlessly fun*?

I've spent much of my life wondering why I don't feel the same joy others seem to feel in their play. When I was in elementary school, my parents purchased a small, used ski boat to putter around our wooded lake. My parents and sisters laughed with joy, the wind in their hair, while I crouched down under the seats to stay warm, terrified we'd flip and drown. My high school friends loved roller coasters, so I dutifully rode them, working my grimace into a grin. And now, an adult heading rapidly toward forty, I was still trying to squeeze myself into a more spontaneous, adrenaline-seeking mold without ever pausing to accept and perhaps even appreciate that I just *wasn't* spontaneous and I flat-out hated adrenaline-inducing activities.

As I thought back to moments of play I enjoyed the most, I began to realize nearly all of them held two things in common: they were quiet, and they were solitary. Reading. Running. Writing. Hiking. Drawing. Sailing. Crossword puzzles. Canoeing. Floating in a pool. For me, happiness is less confetti from a t-shirt cannon and much more like Carl Sandburg's fog that comes in "on little cat feet."[85] I resonate deeply with J. K. Rowling's admission that she is happiest "in a room alone, thinking up ideas."[86] Quiet, contented, peaceful enjoyment is the most playful feeling I know. To that end, many of my happiest childhood memories occurred when my parents left me alone with modeling clay and a book on tape—*Hank the Cowdog*, James Herriot, *Narnia*. In my teen years I graduated to *Tom Bodett* and *The Great Gatsby* and *The History of Saturday Night Live* with the same stash of clay.

The epitome of irritation came when my mom would fetch me to go outside because, in her words, "It's going to be winter before we know it." I knew it. I *loved* winter. No one bothered me to go outside when it was winter. To this day I feel a slight thrill when it's cloudy and rainy or California cold (anything below sixty-five degrees).

"Oh good," my subconscious says, snuggling in with a down comforter, "no boat rides today."

I Googled my favorite brand of shape-and-bake modeling clay from 1992, certain there was no way it'd still be available for purchase in the current year of our Lord. But—joy of joys— it was! I clicked the buy button and felt an immediate rush of delight followed by a nearly-just-as-immediate rush of shame. Modeling clay, really? What was I, *five*? Not to mention I just spent $27.87 that could have been used any number of better ways—groceries, mortgage, near-constant library fines. Lincoln was growing out of all his pants; the car had developed a weird rattle; didn't we want to help Felicity pay for college one day?

Nothing drowns out the winsome invitation of playfulness like a thousand inner voices saying things like, "How *dare* you?"

and "Seriously? *This* is fun for you?" But one the very best parts of adulthood is that we don't have to give the mean kids a voice in our lives anymore; and the voices of Very Practical and Grown Up People Who Like to Remind Us that Things Cost Money™ can speak, but we don't have to listen every time. We don't need to be cool or accept anyone else's definition of what we *should* enjoy one moment longer. We never—and I mean *never*—have to set foot on a roller coaster or a boat again *unless we want to*. We can drive that minivan, listen to that crooner, wear that paisley, you name it. Jenny Joseph's famous poem tells us that when she is old, she shall wear purple, especially if it does not appear on the "must wear" lists of the fashion police of the day.[87]

> IN ADULTHOOD, PLAY BECOMES ALL ABOUT NOTICING, NURTURING, AND GIVING OURSELVES PERMISSION TO FOLLOW OUR JOY.

I'm not giving us permission to be grumps and grouches, ruining everyone else's fun at the theme park or the wharf by pouting while they ride the coasters or sail the seas. I *am* saying that we have a choice. Ownership. A voice. And most of all, permission to investigate our own perfectly playful inner landscapes and discover what's there.

Maybe you, like me, felt happiest as a child when you could create, imagine, or explore on your own. Perhaps you love a big crowd and are energized by playing with others. Maybe you're a planner like I am or a lover of spontaneity like Daryl. There is no right or wrong way to play; our play styles are as unique as we are. In adulthood, play becomes all about noticing, nurturing, and giving ourselves permission to follow our joy.

And my first opportunity was nigh.

At the appointed hour, Daryl gave me a hug and followed it with a high-five.

"What was that for?" I asked.

"Tag," he said. "I'm it. You're off duty. Go play."

Within the hour I was sitting at a kitchen table in an empty house with colorful blocks of clay spread before me. Just the smell of it took me back to afternoons in my parents' basement, the sun streaming through the evergreens, *Hank the Cowdog's* misadventures regaling me from Mom's ancient Boombox. This time I listened to *An Oral History of the Office* without the interruption of our children playing bongo drums or begging for apple slices. I sculpted a pink unicorn and a blue whale, tiny rose earrings and a chubby pig. I mixed colors and squashed them, watching the marbled effects of white and green, yellow and orange, blue and purple.

As my soul settled into the quiet of the house, I felt glimmers of that childhood joy. Creating just to create, for the pure fun of it. The tactile sensations of the clay—squish, roll, shape, smooth—allowed my mind to wander and rest. Uninterrupted thoughts, a body at rest, a chance to breathe deeply in the kind of prayer that is less about words and more about simply *being*.

This dance of noticing, nurturing, and granting ourselves permission is a deeply biblical one. The author of Ecclesiastes puts it this way:

> Seize life! Eat bread with gusto, drink wine with a robust heart. Oh yes—God takes pleasure in *your* pleasure! Dress festively every morning. Don't skimp on colors and scarves. Relish life with the spouse you love each and every day of your precarious life. Each day is God's gift. It's all you get in exchange for the hard work of staying alive. Make the most of each one![88]

The next morning, I woke up craving vegetables, so I ate some chocolate cake just to prove that I could and then took another nap. By afternoon, my clay creations were baking in the oven and I was curled up with the last half of my bedtime novel—one that didn't show up on any lists of Great Books, High Literature, or Must-Reads for the twenty-first century. I read and played and dozed and slowly felt the tight fist inside my soul begin to unclench into an open hand, ready to receive again from God.

Twenty-four hours wasn't nearly enough time to recalibrate my internal compass, but it was a start. A step on the playfulness journey. A reclamation of a child-like way of being that still lived inside me, waiting to spread its wings and give greater strength, courage, and wisdom to my adult self, if I would welcome it back.

I did.

And *that* truly is delightful.

Shooting for the Moon

Almost every month, I pitch a new essay to *The New York Times*. Sometimes it's to their "Rites of Passage" section. Others, it's to "Modern Love." Occasionally it's to the Sunday Review, which is a little bit hilarious because those pages regularly publish Ta-Nahisi Coates and David Brooks and Maureen Dowd and Esau McCaulley, and really, good luck to little ol' me. But taking moon shots is important; otherwise, we'd never have made it to the moon. So I polish my writing and query and query and query some more. My plan is to keep pitching to *The New York Times* until either A) they publish me or B) I die. Parable of the persistent widow and all that.

Though I have a fairly realistic perspective of my own writing abilities (I write from the heart and edit ruthlessly, but no one will hand me a Nobel Prize for literature anytime soon), I can't help but hope that one day I'll open my email box to find a note from the NYT saying they'd *love* to print my work. I have this glimmer of hope each of the approximately 239 times per day I check my email.

"Maybe," I think, opening my inbox.

"Perhaps this time," I murmur, clicking on it twenty minutes later.

"I'll just check once again," I say, logging on before bed, at what would be the wee hours of the morning on the East Coast. It's at this point my hope crosses into unreality. If any NYT editor is up at 3 am, no doubt it's because there is breaking news afoot and *not* because they just really had to send an absolutely not-time-sensitive-email to a first-time contributor who's been flooding their inbox for years.

This practice is silly, exhausting, and utterly unnecessary, yet I can't seem to stop. Hope is a tricky virtue. Emily Dickinson might call it "a thing with feathers," but to me it feels prickly, like a cactus. Sure, it might offer shade in the blazing sun, but watch out for those spines; they show no mercy.

While the Apostle Paul reminds us to be "joyful in hope," this, too, is hard, for often hope forces us to open our hearts in a way that can bring disappointment. How can we hope, knowing we might fail? Between the time I was ready for Daryl to propose and when he actually did, I wrestled with the double-edged sword of hope, wondering if I could survive my shattered heart if he chose a life without me instead. Anyone who has suffered a miscarriage, been left at the altar, grieved a loved one, lost a job or a home, watched their thirties turn to their forties or beyond while waiting to meet "The One," suffered a divorce, lived through a pandemic, or received a devastating diagnosis knows the pain of unfulfilled hope. Anne

Lamott's pastor once told her that the world is basically just a giant emergency ward: "We who are more or less OK for now need to take the tenderest possible care of the more wounded people in the waiting room, until the healer comes."[89]

In light of all the potential loss, we might ask: why on earth should we open ourselves up to such pain? Isn't it wiser to batten down the hatches and let go of whimsy in favor of a more realistic approach to life? Shouldn't we stop hoping and start not hoping in real earnest?

This might be *easier*, but it wouldn't be *better*. Humans are hardwired for hope, programmed for expectant faith. Not because it is pain-free, but because God meets us in these tender, liminal spaces in profound and powerful ways. There are lessons hope teaches that nothing else can: difficult, trying, beautiful, holy lessons. After all, aside from the Psalms, the book of the Bible that speaks most about hope is Job. *Job*. You know, the your-children-are-all-dead-and-you're-covered-in-boils guy.

"Though he slay me, yet will I hope in him," says Job at the height of his misery.[90] He fluctuates between speaking of his hope in God and admitting that his only hope is the grave: a raw, honest portrayal of human emotion in the face of almost unimaginable suffering. Hope is not a feel-good emotion but rather a virtue borne of trust in the One who will one day make all things right. We are called to hope not because we are foolish optimists or silly, pie-in-the-sky people, but because God is who he says he is. Hope is prickly, but perhaps it's less like a cactus and more like a wool sweater—the thick and nubby kind that'll keep you warm in crashing waves, even though you will still get a little bit seasick and a little bit wet.

And as I check my email inbox again, again, again, waiting for word that my essay is *exactly* what they've been looking for and also would I be at all willing to be a regular columnist because *clearly* I am a writer with *extraordinary talents*, I finally begin to ask: who exactly am I hoping in? What exactly am I hoping for?

The answer used to be importance, platform, and a chance to join a broader conversation. I longed to be seen as a valued part of a national discourse. But the older I get, the more that central impulse has shifted to a place of deeper contentment with my local life. Author Laura Lundgren wrote about this same shift happening in her soul: "What if, instead of competing

> HUMANS ARE HARDWIRED FOR HOPE, PROGRAMMED FOR EXPECTANT FAITH.

with other women writers or seeking a larger platform for my writing, I became the 'village poet' for my friends and neighbors and began to see other writers as my peers and friends?"[91] My drive to achieve remains, but now that impulse is growing into an engaging challenge and less of a belief that a certain byline will help me exist in a way that matters. I am learning how much I *already* matter—to my family and friends, to my church and community, to my Jesus.

Now those *New York Times* attempts, as hard as I work to polish those pieces, are *fun*. Even in my craft, I am learning to play.

Because, praise be, God remains, whether or not I ever get published in *The New York Times*. I'll still be just as loved, just as valuable, just as seen by the one who created me. But trying repeatedly—and failing just as often—has helped me hone my craft, raise my bar, polish my prose. Even unfulfilled hope— perhaps unfulfilled hope most of all—can propel us deeper toward Jesus and the happiness he offers.

I check my email again. Nothing. Clearly the Modern Love folks are playing hard to get.

I'll try again.

ACCEPT THE INVITATION
Fail Regularly

1. Read Acts 16:16–35. How do Paul and Silas's actions get them in trouble? From the outside, this might look like failure; their message lands them in prison. Yet God uses it to bring incredible good to the jailer and his family. Where has God brought good out of a perceived failure in your life?

2. What is one thing you want to do but haven't because you fear failing at it? What's holding you back? What might it be like to give that thing a try?

3. What are some of the hidden graces of failure? How can failure help draw us closer to Jesus? How can failure be playful?

4. This chapter encourages us to "fail often," not just once in a while. How can repeated failure help free us for greater playfulness and creativity?

5. If perfection isn't the goal, then what is?

10

Take Off Your Shoes

Throughout Christian history, Christian worship
has been a profoundly sensuous experience, a
training ground for pleasure and delight.
—TISH HARRISON WARREN

Years ago, Daryl and I attended an Easter Eve service at an Anglican church outside Chicago. We'd been invited by a friend who couldn't stop gushing about how moving and beautiful the service would be, of the ways God might meet us there.

"Oh, and also," he said, almost as an afterthought, "it's five hours long. So bring snacks."

"Five hours?!" I said to Daryl after the friend went home. "Is he off his rocker?" Yet we were young, and it was Lent in the frozen prairies of the Midwest where there is not much to do but eat ice cream and read novels and wait for the spring thaw to come; so we went, sitting in the flip-down seats of a high

school auditorium with other worshipers who'd come in from the cold to welcome the risen Christ.

The first hours of the service were measured and somber. The drama team reenacted the story of creation, the beauty of God's good world and then the devastation of humanity's fall. A tenor sang the story of God's plan of salvation from Isaiah. We knelt to confess our sins. We stood and raised our voices together in hymns.

The lights were dimmed. Though the service wasn't dragging, as the hours turned over and over, I was aware of my backside growing numb and my attention span beginning to flag.

Then came the retelling of the death of Christ. People wailed. The dim sanctuary went completely dark. Lent in the freezing cold of Illinois is somber enough; the last thing I really wanted to do was feel bad for my sins when I'd been feeling crummy enough after barely seeing the sun for three months.

I get it, Jesus, I prayed. *We are bad. It is dark. It's our fault. We're sorry.*

It wasn't that I wasn't penitent; I'd been thinking a lot about not only my own sins, which were many, but the corporate and systemic sins it was nearly impossible *not* to participate in as a Western Christian. Who knew who'd sewn the shirt I was wearing and whether they'd been paid a decent wage? How could I fill my car with gas without participating in some of the world's deadliest conflicts over oil? Which people groups had been displaced centuries ago so I could live in the rich farmlands of the Midwest?

But I was tired, too. Tired of my sin. Tired of myself. Tired of the endless cycle of repentance and forgiveness and trying hard and failing again. Lent is *long*. Just then the senior priest ran on stage from the wings of the chancel holding a large bell, his curly hair a muss. He paused at the center of the stage for a split second and then yelled out, his eyes wildly ablaze, "JESUS. IS. RISEN."

The congregation erupted. Shouts of joy reverberated from every row. Noisemakers appeared from purses and backpacks, and people began to play tambourines and flutes and maracas. The woman a couple rows in front of us began clanging—I kid you not—a *cowbell*.

"What is *happening*?" I hissed to Daryl, my quiet, Protestant church self braced for a riot.

"It's the holy noise!" he announced, pointing to a note in the bulletin. Sure enough, after reading passages about the death of Christ and silent prayer came—of all things—the holy noise. The worship band struck up a lilting rendition of the David Ruis song "We Will Dance," and the entire auditorium swelled in song. I felt a tug at my sleeve—a preteen beckoned me.

"Dance with us?" she asked.

When I hesitated, Daryl was out into the aisle in a flash, joining a jubilant conga line of children and college students and teenagers that wove its way up and down the aisles. On his second pass by our row, I joined him.

As the people of God belted out choruses and hymns, for the first time in my life I danced in church, running up and down the aisles with the youth group, sweat springing up on our foreheads as the lay leaders carried hyacinths and fragrant lilies out from the wings to fill the altar and the stairs with color and scent and life.

PLAYFULNESS INVITES US TO WORSHIP GOD FREELY AND FULLY. WE ARE INVITED TO STAND BEFORE GOD KNOWING THAT HE IS THE ONE WHO MAKES ORDINARY THINGS—AND ORDINARY PEOPLE, LIKE US!—HOLY.

I lost Daryl somewhere in the flow of dancers, his hand pulled from mine, but it didn't matter. The dance was there for all of us, for each of us. We were one in the joy of the resurrection, the celebration of new life, the pulse-pounding reel. Step by step I began to forget myself, gripping the hand of the boy in front of me and the girl in back in a cavalcade of joy. Blood pumped in my ears. The band played on.

Collapsing back into our seats a few songs later, glistening and disheveled, neither Daryl nor I could wipe the smiles from our faces.

"Was that *okay?*" I asked him, a little afraid someone had caught me on video, and even more afraid that we may have accidentally joined a cult. Surely this much happiness couldn't be appropriate for worship, could it?

"Celebrating the resurrection of Jesus by dancing?" he responded. "Uh, yeah, pretty sure that's not only okay, it's *necessary.*"

He had a point. If the story of God is true, *really* true—if there truly is hope beyond our wildest dreams, a Savior whose love is more powerful than death, grace to forgive our worst sins, and healing to transform our most broken places—then how can we keep from dancing?

Psalms of Permission

Worship is an inherently playful act. We approach God with open hands, waiting for the movement of the Spirit, the invitations of grace, the rhythms of confession and repentance, restoration and transformation. The Christian life is much less an exercise in rule-following and much more a dance where God leads and we learn stumblingly, haltingly, and eventually even gracefully, to follow.

The Psalms are one of the most playful texts of Scripture. Rather than history or narrative, they are poetry, song, chant, metaphor. Though they are rarely taught as a prayer book in the modern Protestant church, they are our oldest records of the people of God at prayer. When I read them as a child, then in college, and later in seminary, I always read with an attempt to understand and parse them. What did it *mean* that the Lord was my shepherd? What did it *mean* that I would want for nothing? I tried to wring out their essence, learn their lessons, and figure out what they wanted me to *do*. It wasn't until I came to the end of my own words that I began to see them for what they were—not prescriptive rules but invitations to a life of prayer.

The Psalms are raw. Messy. In some places, they are violent and bordering on unhinged. They pulse with grief, frustration, rage, and rejoicing. They don't tell us *how* to pray; they show us what it looks like to bring our whole selves to God in prayer. Suddenly, speaking with God isn't about saying the right things in the proper way but instead about feeling our feelings in God's presence and letting him deeply adore us while also working in and on and through us. The Psalms provide a beautiful, playful release, even in times of great suffering.

I began to let the ancient words of Scripture become my prayers when I didn't know what to say to God or how to say it. It surprised me how often they gave voice to the depths of my pain or longing or rage or need. "How long, O Lord?" in the seemingly unending days of morning sickness. "The nations rage and the people plot in vain," as I worried over the world afire. "For my sin is always before me," when I snapped at the kids over something that didn't remotely warrant snapping and then didn't ever apologize because *I so didn't want to.*

The long, winding Psalms became grace in their duration alone. When reading long passages, I couldn't pin down every single word and figure out *what it meant.* I had to just let the words wash over me, reading them aloud in the silence of my room, my office, my car. If the Holy Spirit prays for us with "groans too deep for words," the Psalms often gave a written voice to my groaning. I began learning how to offer these permission-filled words to others, too.

> THE PSALMS PROVIDE A BEAUTIFUL, PLAYFUL RELEASE, EVEN IN TIMES OF GREAT SUFFERING.

Many years ago, a woman came to see me who was struggling with feelings too big for her to feel safe in their midst. [92] In my office, she poured out the story of an errant son-in-law who, embroiled in substance abuse and a messy divorce from her daughter, got drunk and kidnapped her grandson, holding him captive with a gun to the young boy's head. Mercifully, the police tracked them down in time and were able to calm him. No shots were fired, but the grandson's trauma rocked the family to its core.

I knew the story—it'd been in the local paper—but hearing it retold chilled me. Things could have ended so differently, and even with the "happy" ending, the fallout would last a lifetime.

"I *hate* him," she said. "I hate him for what he did to my grandson and my daughter. I hate that he could do it again when he gets out of prison. I hate that he isn't sorry. I hate him so much it keeps me up at night. But Christians shouldn't hate anyone, right?" She sat quietly, defeated, tears running down her face. "What am I supposed to do?"

Just days earlier I'd read a Psalm I couldn't find my own way into, struggling to make sense of its rage. It describes the fall of Jerusalem and the brutal retribution suffered by God's people. It ends violently and on a horrific note. But I realized—if a child dear to me had been held at gunpoint, this would have been exactly the Psalm I needed.

I opened to Psalm 137, and we read it together.

"It's a prayer," I said.

"Can ... can I *pray* that?" she asked.

"It's in the Bible," I said. She was silent for a moment. "You can bring these feelings to God," I said. "He isn't afraid of them. He is big enough to handle them. And he will do what is right." Her shoulders softened.

"I can tell God that I hate my son-in-law and don't want to forgive him?" she asked.

"You can," I said.

"But doesn't God want me to forgive him?"

"He does," I said. "But God never calls us to invite violence back into our lives. You can forgive from a distance. And if you keep close to God, he will bring you there at a pace you can handle." She paused, looking down at her hands.

"Can we read it again?"

Happy Are We

The Psalms are an intense and beautiful school for prayer, but all of Scripture rings out with lessons of worship and connection. I once heard a pastor preach on the beatitudes: blessed are the meek, the poor in spirit, those who mourn.

"Did you know," he asked the congregation, "the Greek word for *blessed* can also be translated *happy?*"

"There's no way that's true," I whispered to the guy sitting next to me. The one I'd end up marrying years later. The one I'd met in introductory Greek class because we were a very similar brand of nerd. After worship, we grabbed a Greek/English dictionary and—burgeoning scholars that we were—did some research.

"My gosh," Daryl said, "he's right!" We'd both so taken it to heart that God was concerned with our holiness over our happiness that we'd never stopped to discern whether or not that was even true. It turns out that God's profoundly interested in the happiness of his creation; and the full spectrum of human flourishing includes not just goodness and obedience but delight as well. And as Andrew Peterson so perfectly puts it, "We're not invited into this because God needs us, but because he *wants* us."[93]

The difference between the happiness God offers and the happiness our culture so often trumpets is that God knows the path that can get us to joy. It isn't in accumulating or power-grabbing, sex or money, comfort or abundance. It's in him. "Happy are the poor" only makes sense in the economy of God. But then, he has the map.

Thou Shalt Play

For a book with a reputation among many for being stuffed with stuffy rules, do's and do not's, the Bible is almost shockingly filled with instructions about how, where, and when to celebrate. God is, it seems, quite dedicated to teaching his creation about joy. Knowing the human propensity for seriousness over delight and angst over joy, from the earliest pages of Scripture God writes celebration into his divine word.

After creating the heavens and the earth, God rests—an inherently trusting and playful act. The book of Exodus lists three required observances centered around seasons of the year: the Festival of Unleavened Bread, the Festival of Harvest, and the Festival of Ingathering. The first reminded the people of God of their deliverance from Egypt; the second allowed them to pause during a busy season, offering the very first of their crops to God; and the third celebration centered around the gathering in of the main harvest.[94] (If it's confusing to you that the Festival of Harvest wasn't about the final harvest of the crops, I get it. I didn't write the rules.) During each one, God's people were reminded to pause from their everyday tasks, turn to him and one another, and celebrate his goodness. Over and over again God says, "Stop. Look up. Remember. Trust."

Later in Exodus, the Festival of Weeks is added. By Leviticus, the number of festivals has grown to seven, along with five prescribed feasts, including the Day of Atonement.[95] In Numbers, we read of monthly "new moon" feast days.[96] Later, Purim—the celebration of God's deliverance of the Jews from destruction, written about in Esther—is added, as is Chanukah, which celebrates the restoration of the temple in 164 B.C.[97] And each of these is in *addition* to the weekly celebration of Sabbath. These communal rituals of feast and festival united the people of God in worship and celebration and flowed with the ancient agricultural calendar as a constant reminder of God as "provider and sustainer."[98]

These celebrations are another way playfulness is written into Scripture's moral code. Pausing to remember and thank God, the source of joy and blessing, is not suggested but *required*. Even in the days of the Old Testament, people were more prone to work than play, so God arranged for regular rhythms of rest and worship, from weekly Sabbaths to consistent feasts. Though their work would always remain unfinished, their

Lord could be trusted all the same. Each festival required a tangible remembering of God's goodness.

At the Festival of Unleavened Bread, for example, God's people were instructed to eat bread without yeast for seven full days as an edible expression of their shared history of deliverance from slavery and oppression in Egypt. Each inbreaking of festivity offered opportunity to retell the stories of God's care and concern, reorienting the people's gaze heavenward in adoration and love.

The celebrations continue in the New Testament. We read of Jesus observing them, traveling to his hometown or to the temple in Jerusalem. He feasts with friends, takes his time at the table, and participates with his community. Even when Jesus is in great danger, he still attends these worshipful celebrations. John 7 describes how he quietly made his way to the Festival of Tabernacles: "After his brothers had left for the festival, he went also, not publicly, but in secret."[99]

These rituals continued throughout the New Testament and into the years beyond. By medieval times, the European church featured *two hundred* feast days every year, with more than half of the days in the calendar dedicated to celebrations big or small.[100] Today, even the most ascetic Catholic traditions celebrate regular festivals as a sign of God's goodness, provision, and love.

A Congregation at Play

For most of us today, the celebrations of the church have melded a bit with the celebrations of culture. The pews are fullest on Easter Sunday and second-fullest on Christmas Eve, but the next biggest Sunday is Mother's Day,[101] not a traditional Christian holiday like Palm Sunday or All Saints Day. I've heard preachers tut-tut over this as the secularization of the church, the creeping in of the world, the acquiescence of thousands of years of Christian tradition to the whims of capitalism. They have a point. Still, I'm more comfortable standing on the side of celebration.

If our culture wants to celebrate, surely the church is the place people should come to connect with God in their joy. While we may not celebrate two hundred feasts any longer, we can acknowledge cultural holidays at every point they connect with our great tradition. Martin Luther King Jr.'s birthday has much to remind us about the hope of racial justice—and how far we have yet to come. Halloween is tied to All Soul's Day, remembering our loved ones who have died in the faith. Even Valentine's Day can be a reminder to look to the singles, widows, and widowers in our midst and make sure they are folded in with love.

Our senior pastor, Jackson, is a master at playfulness. When our church staff gets stuck in a rut, he'll cancel our regular meeting and take us to a bowling alley, an escape room, a coffee shop.

"If this isn't *fun*, then what's the point?" he asked me once, noticing my furrowed brow over a packet of spreadsheets. Don't get me wrong—he's a scholar, a leader, and a peacemaker, too. He works *incredibly* hard; it's just that he also understands that the work of God can't always be shoved into a box. Sometimes we all need to get out of our heads and play before we can begin to notice what God is up to.

In Exodus, Moses is taking care of his father-in-law's sheep. He's fallen a long way from his place of honor in the courts of Pharaoh. Now he's nothing but a shepherd. His days are hot and long and quiet. The work is smelly and mundane. And then he notices it—a fire in the bush. Not a wholly unusual sight: lightning sometimes struck; fires sometimes sprang up. And yet, this one is different.

Moses studies it. The fire burns and burns, but the bush remains the same. It is not consumed. It is not changed. Slowly, Moses walks closer. And then it happens.

"Moses!" the bush calls.

Moses answers, "Here I am."

"Do not come any closer," says the Lord (for of course, it is he). "Take off your sandals, for the place where you are standing is holy."[102]

Take off your shoes. Go ahead, I'll wait.

The place where *you* are standing is holy. That's right. Your bedroom floor or the parquet of the coffee shop or the patio tile or the floor mats below the passenger's seat or the carpet at the dentist's office. The ground is holy. So is the air. So are your hands and feet, your home and office, your very breath.

God has come down to bring us life. To give us grace. To renew our spirits. Over and over again in Scripture, God says to his beloved, "As I was with Moses, so I will be with you."

> SOMETIMES WE ALL NEED TO GET OUT OF OUR HEADS AND PLAY BEFORE WE CAN BEGIN TO NOTICE WHAT GOD IS UP TO.

As we find our way, once again, into our native country of joy, God is all around. Waking us up. Settling us down. Opening our hands and our eyes. Reminding us that we are his children.

Turning up the volume.

Teaching us jazz.

ACCEPT THE INVITATION
Take Off Your Shoes

1. Read Exodus 3:1–10. Why did Moses have to take off his shoes? What does it mean to stand upon holy ground?

2. To be holy means to be "set apart." How does God set us apart? Where in your life do you feel closest to the holiness of God?

3. Have you ever experienced a worship service like the Easter Eve service described here? If not, what would it be like to seek out a new experience like this? Is there a church in your area where you could visit to worship in a different style?

4. Do you agree that a church that plays together will stay together? Why or why not? Have you ever experienced play at church? What difference did it make for you?

5. What does it mean to "learn jazz"? How might Jesus be inviting you into a jazzier way of life?

Epilogue

"**C**an we make a water park?" Wilson asked me, leaning his rosy-cheeked grin between my face and my computer screen. "In the backyard?"

There were roughly sixty thousand reasons to say no. Our sprinkler was broken. I had so much work to do. It was the end of our second month of stay-at-home orders. Every time I turned on the news I was greeted with new information about infection rates, death numbers, and global unrest. Pastoring our church through a season of such tumult and uncertainty regularly took *all* of me, and Daryl's pastoral load was just as heavy. The struggle of distance learning was soul-crushing for Lincoln and for us. (Ask me if I would have put our firstborn into a Spanish immersion public school if I knew it'd mean helping him learn Common Core math *in a language I do not speak?!* Go ahead. Ask me.) To say I was plumb out of creative energy would be quite an understatement. Try tuberculosis-tired and not a little shell-shocked.

On top of it all, it was a chilly day for California, and I knew the kids would only be happy in the sprinkler for a short while before the shivering and complaining began.

But reader, I'd learned a few things in the writing of this book. I'd learned that rest is essential but that sometimes, playing can be its own kind of rest. I'd learned to accept invitations to connect, treating play attempts as the tender and precious things they are. I'd learned to give myself permission to be less productive, less driven, less nose-to-the-grindstone. I'd discovered I wasn't too old for adventure, that investing in people was never *not* a good idea, that even useless things had deeply important use, and that the ground I stood on—even the Lego-strewn, crayon-scribbled faux wood of my living room—was holy.

I took a breath.

"Sure!" I said. I didn't feel playful. Not in the least. But emotions are educable, and playfulness has a way of infusing its own joy and energy once we've accepted its invitation.

And do you know what? As I hooked up the hose to a makeshift olive oil bottle sprinkler (MacGyver has nothing on the modern mom) and the kids stripped down to their skivvies, my worn soul paused for its first deep breath in many a day. The kids broke into grins. God began remaking the whole world, right in our little square of earth.

At first, I followed Felicity around the yard, but then she told me with a stern, brow-furrowed glare that I was crowding her. So I turned on our dance mix and spun around with my eyes to the cloudy sky, just me and Jesus in the delight of motion and movement and freedom, spinning in the blessed and terrifying uncertainty of hope, in the corner of the same backyard we'd spent the last fifty-six days together in, releasing my fears to the sky and listening to the magical laughter—and periodic bickering, let's be honest—of the three little people who call me Mom.

Thank you, Jesus, I prayed.

I had no idea what would come next. In that season nearly everything about the world—and our little corner of it— seemed uncertain. Yet I rejoiced that, as Wendell Berry put it in his Sabbath Poems, "If tonight the world ends, we'll have had this day."[103]

In that moment, I knew I was loved and cherished and known and free. In that moment, I found myself singing.

And if that's not a metaphor for the entire abundant Christian life, I don't know what is.

So here is what I know: I am on the road to happiness. I visit it more often than I did and stay there longer than I used to. The fastest way there is through a playful spirit, but that requires our basic needs to be met. We need Sabbath rest and safety, love and nourishment, invitation and permission. Then all we need is to let ourselves go there, trusting that God will meet us.

He always has.

I believe he always will.

Acknowledgments

Thank you to the wonderful team at Hendrickson Rose, especially Cristalle Kishi, Sergio Urquiza, Glen Andrews, Raechel Wong, Meg Rusick, Maggie Swofford, Maria Morales-Gordon, John Ribeiro, and, of course, Paul Hendrickson. You folks are talented beyond all comprehension, and I count it an honor to write for you. To Lynnette Pennings, Managing Editor extraordinaire, master of encouragement, you have made this entire process a joy, and I hope to write many more books with you. To Kay Ben-Avraham, kind and faithful editor, who makes me sound smarter, holier, funnier, and wiser than I really am, all while making me laugh. To my publicist, Don Otis. And to Bob Hostetler, agent and friend, who tells it like it is but always in the kindest way.

Thank you to April Rudge and Twyla Zerwas for becoming my volunteer research assistants. To Ann Bergen for all her wisdom in helping young people rediscover their playful spirits. To Jacob Robinson for introducing me to the concept of holy leisure. To Jackson and Malaika Clelland for their knowledge of play, and for how freely they share it. To Dakota Shyres for taking me cycling, Matt Becerra and Jeff Given for beating me in Scrabble (feel free to let me win one of these times), John Lam and Kierlynn Densham for bringing me to the archery range, and Kassy Najm for being willing to take me surfing, even if I keep being too scared to actually go.

Thank you to the Simons, Cutkomps, Weilers, Swetnams, Bohms, Robertsons, Wright-Bushmans, Givens, Pacinis, Wheatley-Blumhofers, and Ericksons, for being friends who live in pursuit of holy play. To Maddi Hundley, who has become part of our little fam. I forgive you for taking me on that Black Diamond—it was an adventure!

To Bethany Rydmark, Moriah Conant, and Jennifer Robinson for being fabulous beta readers. To the rest of my writerly heroes and friends: Susan Baller-Shepherd, Bethany Beams, Dorcas Cheng-Tozun, Rebecca Cochran, Sarah Cozart, Andi Cumbo-Floyd, Marvia Davidson, Aarik Danielsen, Chara Donahue, Gail Dudley, April Emick Fiet, Katy Epling, Ruth Everhart, John Graeber, Marlena Graves, Elizabeth Hagan, Harmony Harkema, Dana Herndon, Carol Howard Merritt, Collin Huber, Amy Joy Ickes, Stephanie Jenkins, Alia Joy, Kathy Khang, Kristen Joy Kludt, Stephanie Lobdell, Catherine McNeil, Holly Oxhandler, Paul J. Pastor, Rebecca Peet, Jen Pollock Michel, Sarah Quezada, KJ Ramsey, Traci Rhoades, Jill Richardson, Sara Sanderson, Lisa Scandrette, Kelly Smith, Shawn Smucker, Andrea Stunz, Karen Swallow Prior, Gena Thomas, Michelle van Loon, Leslie Verner, Robert Vore, Chris Upham, Amber Wackford, Beth Walker, Megan Westra, and Melissa Wilkins, whose encouragement as fellow-writers-in-the-trenches lifts me. To Cara Meredith for the disco ball. To my writing cohorts—Grammatical Foibles, The Chapter, and For the Love—bless you for being such friends on the journey. And to the crew of Fathom Mag, for being so consistently lovely.

To our dear neighbors, the Nichols family—Adam, Terri, Aubrey, Elizabeth, David, Peter, Mary, and Lillian; to Frank and Bertha; Jeff and Dawn; Lucy and Brad; Mike and Susie; Bob and Trish; Ben and Negin; Bob and Pat; Brian, Fern, and Kyle; John, Grant, and Tara; Chris, MaryKen, and Dusay; Dale, Chris, and Cooper, and all the kiddos. Neighborhood play is some of the very best.

To Presbyterian Church of the Master: thank you for leading the way in holy laughter, for embracing me as your pastor and storyteller, and for reminding me that worshiping with open hands can change the world. Thank you to my fellows in ministry at PCOM: Dianne, Sue, Sara, Carol, Kelly, Cynthia, Anda, Dee, Matt, Dakota, Jeff, Stephanie, Vanessa, Kristin, Alyona, Fran, José, Gene, Kathy, Jenna, Isaac, Dan, Anna, Tom, John, the other John, and Jackson.

To Anna Woofenden, Sonia Justl Ellis, Alicia Akins, Inga Wildermuth, Anna Thelen and Bethany Erickson for being such dear soul friends and brilliant women of faith. By serving as my Marco Polo posse, you've offered heaps of encouragement, wisdom, and kindness, and continual reminders that no one can walk this Jesus road alone. I'd be lost without each and every one of you.

To my Ellis family—Sylvia, your gentle wisdom helped shape this book; Tad, between your puns and your pies, you've passed on wonderfully playful treasure to us; Deborah, your literary friendship is a gift. Jill and Judd, letting us escape to your pool during the height of our Covid summer saved our good humor and our sanity. Dave, Emily, and Taylor, we can't wait to hit up Legoland with you again.

To my Snick family—Grandpa, thank you for teaching me that solitude is its own gift. Grandma, thank you for lessons in how dollar store items can keep kids happily playing for hours! (Scotch tape! Who knew?)

To my Belcher family—Grandma, thank you for being such a wonderful early editor; and Grandpa, thank you for your faithfulness in modeling what it is to follow Jesus even on the eve of brain surgery. Thank you, above all, for your consistent prayers.

To my sisters—Caitlyn, you will forever be more fun than I am, but at least I'm finally admitting it. Caroline, I owe you a picture of the two of us with Peter Pan and Tinkerbell! Come back to California, and we will make it happen. Michael and Jared—you are the best brothers-in-law a girl could ask for. To all my Belcher nieces and nephews—Aleah, Sophia, Hudson, Haven, Arlo, and Pippa, you are just the coolest people. I love watching you grow.

Mom and Dad, thank you for filling my childhood home with music, art, and ice hockey, and for giving my sisters and me permission to create, experiment, fail, and create again. Thank you, too, for all your help with the kidlets—this book would still be in pieces if it wasn't for their hours at "Camp Grandma Grandpa."

To my dear, dear kiddos, Lincoln, Wilson, and Felicity. Thank you for inviting me to play with you, even when I am just trying to write *one... more... sentence.* You are each unique and incredible delights, and I can't believe I get to witness the miracles you are.

To Daryl, the most deep, tender, caring, and seriously silly person I've ever met, for walking alongside me as a friend on the journey, and occasionally putting on a dinosaur mask just to make me smile. Thank you for diving back into play with me. Same team, always.

To you, dear reader, for rediscovering playfulness with me.

And to Jesus, for teaching me, slowly and patiently and surely, that it's not only okay but beautiful to play jazz.

Notes

PART I

Chapter 1

1   Hobbes, *Leviathan*, 76.
2   1 Peter 1:24.
3   Public Domain, "Be Thou My Vision."
4   Brown, *Play*, 33.
5   Maslow, "A Theory of Human Motivation."
6   Malaika Clelland, personal interview, November 12, 2019.
7   Barragan, "Inside Google's Cool New Playa Vista Offices," and Avalos, "Facebook's Striking New Menlo Park Building."
8   Gray, *Free to Learn*, 139.
9   Raz, "Khan Academy: Sal Khan."
10 Einstein, "Letter to Hans Muehsam," 404.
11 Gay, *The Book of Delights*, 163.
12 Matthew 9:12.

Chapter 2

13 Psalm 13:1.
14 Nancherla, *Twitter*.
15 Brooks, "Are We Trading Our Happiness for Modern Comforts?"
16 Ray, "Americans' Stress."
17 Brooks, "Are We Trading Our Happiness for Modern Comforts?"
18 Griffith, "Why Are Young People Pretending to Love Work?"
19 Brown, *Play*, 64.
20 Bergen, "Career, Vocation, College and Faith."
21 United States Bureau of Labor Statistics, "American Time Use Survey."
22 Rubin, "Theme Index."
23 Gough, "Total NBA Revenue."
24 United States Bureau of Labor Statistics, "Consumer Expenditures 2018."

25   "2019 Global Emotions Report," *Gallup.*

26   Woofenden, *This Is God's Table*, 132.

27   Friedman, *A Failure of Nerve*, 64.

28   John 3:5–6 (MSG).

29   Aarik Danielsen, personal endorsement for *Happy Now.*

30   Chris Blumhofer, personal correspondence, September 5, 2019.

31   Brown, *Play*, 71.

Chapter 3

32   Brown, *Dare to Lead*, 81.

33   Holley, "Wynton Marsalis."

34   Norris, "Luke 14: A Commentary," 239.

PART II

Chapter 1

35   Jenkins, "Drink It In."

36   Center for Disease Control, "1 in 3 Adults."

37   Perez, "U. S. Adults."

38   Lee, "People Spend More Time."

39   Muller, *Sabbath*, 1 (emphasis mine).

40   Wendell Berry, as quoted in Davis, *Scripture*, 66.

41   Davis, "Working from Home."

42   Brueggemann, *Sabbath as Resistance*, 18–19.

43   Wendell Berry, as quoted in Davis, *Scripture*, 66, emphasis mine.

44   Peterson, *Tell It Slant*, 82.

45   Peterson, *Working the Angles*, 70.

46   Barton, *Sacred Rhythms*, 133.

47   Heschel, *The Sabbath*, vii.

48   Mark 2:27 (NRSV).

Chapter 2

49   Smucker, "Dad, I Love This Day."

50   Junod, "My Friend Mr. Rogers."

51   Dillard, *Pilgrim at Tinker Creek*, 17.

52   Gay, *The Book of Delights*, xii.

53   Matthew 18:3.

54 Dickinson, "Time and Eternity."
55 Bianichi, "Mary Budd Rowe."
56 Tugwell, "Prayer," 324.
57 Paul, "Let Children Get Bored."
58 Miller, "The Relentlessness."
59 Elkind, *The Power of Play*, 85.
60 Gray, *Free to Learn*, 18.
61 Psalm 36:8.

Chapter 3

62 Gottman, *The Seven Principles*, 27.
63 Akins, "Single Ladies' Catechism."
64 Tugwell, *Prayer*, vii.

Chapter 4

65 John 3:8 (NET).

Chapter 5

66 Milne, *The Complete Tales of Winnie-the-Pooh*, 77.
67 Matthew 11:17–19 (MSG).
68 Matthew 26:13.
69 John 2:3, 10.

Chapter 6

70 Names and some identifying details have been changed in this story.
71 Dillard, *Teaching a Stone to Talk*, 25.
72 Genesis 12:4.
73 Karl Barth, quoted in Fitzhenry, *The Harper Book of Quotations*, 223.

Chapter 7

74 Nicolaus, "Want to Feel Happier Today?"
75 Okoro, *Silence*, 92.
76 Isaiah 30:21.
77 Sonia Justl Ellis, personal correspondence, April 18, 2019.
78 Davis, "A Half-Century After 'Mister Rogers' Debut."

Chapter 8

79   Cohen, *Playful Parenting*, 287.
80   Foster, *A Celebration of Discipline*, 31.

Chapter 9

81   2 Corinthians 12:9.
82   O'Connor, "The Fiction Writer," 35.
83   Taylor, "How Coca-Cola."
84   Gay, *The Book of Delights*, 142–3.
85   Sandburg, "Fog," 37.
86   Rowling, author biography.
87   Joseph, *Warning*, 1.
88   Ecclesiastes 9:9–10a (MSG).
89   Lamott, *Traveling Mercies*, 106.
90   Job 13:15.
91   Lundgren, "Plugged in to the Vine."

Chapter 10

92   Identifying details have been changed to protect the privacy of those involved.
93   Peterson, *Adorning the Dark*, 33.
94   Exodus 23.
95   Walton, *Chronological and Background Charts*, 20.
96   Numbers 10:10, 28:11–15.
97   Walton, *Chronological and Background Charts*, 20.
98   Hill and Walton, *A Survey of the Old Testament*, 109.
99   John 7:10.
100 Seah, "Taking Back Sundays."
101 Stetzer, "Brand New Research."
102 Exodus 3:1–10.

Epilogue

103 Berry, "After the Long Weeks," 393.

Bibliography

Allady, Meredith. *Letters to Julia: The Merriweather Chronicles.* CreateSpace Independent Publishing, 2014.

Akins, Alicia. "Single Ladies Catechism." *Feet Cry Mercy.* February 13, 2019. https://feetcrymercy.com/2019/02/13/single-ladies-catechism (Retrieved July 1, 2020).

Avalos, George. "Facebook's striking new Menlo Park building akin to village with office neighborhoods." *The Mercury News.* September 4, 2018. https://www.mercurynews.com/2018/09/04/facebooks-striking-new-menlo-park-building-akin-to-village-with-office-neighborhoods.

Barragan, Bianca. "Inside Google's cool new Playa Vista offices." *Curbed LA.* November 8, 2018. https://la.curbed.com/2018/11/8/18075714/google-playa-vista-offices-photos-spruce-goose.

Barton, Ruth Haley. *Sacred Rhythms: Arranging Our Lives for Spiritual Transformation.* Downers Grove, IL: Intervarsity Press, 2006.

Bergen, Ann. "Career, Vocation, College, and Faith with Ann Bergen." *The PCOM Podcast.* September 10, 2019.

Berry, Wendell. "After the long weeks," *This Day.* Berkeley: Counterpoint, 2013.

Bianichi, Julie A. "Mary Budd Rowe: A storyteller of science." *Cultural Studies of Science Education* 3(4): 799–810. December 2008.

Blumhofer, Chris. Personal correspondence. September 5, 2019.

Brooks, Arthur C. "Are We Trading Our Happiness for Modern Comforts? As society gets richer, people chase the wrong things." *The Atlantic.* October 22, 2020. https://www.theatlantic.com/family/archive/2020/10/why-life-has-gotten-more-comfortable-less-happy/616807 (Retrieved October 24, 2020).

Brown, Brené. *Dare to Lead*. New York: Penguin Random House, 2018.

Brown, Brené. *The Gifts of Imperfection*. Center City, MN: Hazelden, 2010.

Brown, Stuart. *Play: How it Shapes the Brain, Opens the Imagination, and Invigorates the Soul*. New York: Penguin Random House, 2009.

Brueggemann, Walter. *Sabbath as Resistance: Saying No in a Culture of Now*. Louisville, KY: Westminster John Knox, 2017.

Center for Disease Control. "1 in 3 Adults Don't Get Enough Sleep." https://www.cdc.gov/media/releases/2016/p0215-enough-sleep. html (Retrieved January 5, 2020).

Clelland, Malaika. Personal interview. November 12, 2019.

Cohen, Lawrence J. *Playful Parenting: A Bold New Way to Nurture Close Connections, Solve Behavior Problems, and Encourage Children's Confidence*. New York: Ballantine Books, 2001.

Danielsen, Aarik. Endorsement for *Happy Now*.

Davis, Ellen F. *Scripture, Culture, and Agriculture*. New York: Cambridge University Press, 2009.

Davis, Leslie and Kim Parker. "A half-century after 'Mister Rogers' debut, 5 facts about neighbors in U.S." *Pew Research Center*. August 15, 2019. https://www.pewresearch.org/fact-tank/2019/08/15/facts-about-neighbors-in-u-s (Retrieved February 18, 2020).

Davis, Michelle F. "Working from Home in COVID Era Means Three More Hours." *Bloomberg*. April 23, 2020. https://www.bloomberg. com/news/articles/2020-04-23/working-from-home-in-covid-era-means-three-more-hours-on-the-job (Retrieved June 30, 2020).

Dickinson, Emily. "Time and Eternity." *The Complete Poems of Emily Dickinson*. New York: Little Brown, 1960.

Dillard, Annie. *Pilgrim at Tinker Creek*. New York: HarperCollins, 2013.

Dillard, Annie. *Teaching a Stone to Talk: Expeditions and Encounters*. New York: Harper & Row, 1982.

Einstein, Albert. "Letter to Hans Muehsam. July 9, 1951." *Einstein Archives* quoted in *The Ultimate Quotable Einstein* by Alice Calprice, 2010.

Elkind, David. *The Power of Play*. Philadelphia: Da Capo Press, 2007.

Ellis, Sonia Justl. Personal correspondence. April 18, 2019.

Fitzhenry, Robert I. *The Harper Book of Quotations*. New York: Collins Reference, 1993.

Foster, Richard J. *Celebration of Discipline*. New York: HarperCollins, 1998.

Friedman, Edwin H. *A Failure of Nerve: Leadership in the Age of the Quick Fix*. Greenwich, CT: Seabury Books, 2017.

Full Psychle. Full Psychle online waiver. South County location (Retrieved September 23, 2019).

Gallup. "2019 Global Emotions Report." https://www.gallup.com/ analytics/248906/gallup-global-emotions-report-2019.aspx (Retrieved February 20, 2020).

Gay, Ross. *The Book of Delights*. Chapel Hill, NC: Algonquin Books of Chapel Hill, 2019.

Gottman, John. *The Seven Principles for Making Marriage Work*. New York: Harmony Books, 2015.

Gough, Christina. "Total NBA revenue 2001–2018." *Statista*. https:// www.statista.com/statistics/193467/total-league-revenue-of-the-nba-since-2005 (Retrieved February 20, 2020).

Gray, Peter. *Free to Learn: Why Unleashing the Instinct to Play Will Make Our Children Happier, More Self-Reliant, and Better Students for Life*. New York: Basic Books, 2013.

Griffith, Erin. "Why Are Young People Pretending to Love Work?" *The New York Times*. January 26, 2019. https://www.nytimes. com/2019/01/26/business/against-hustle-culture-rise-and-grind-tgim.html (Retrieved February 21, 2019).

Heschel, Abraham Joshua. *The Sabbath*. New York: Farrar, Straus, and Giroux, 1951.

Higgins, Maeve. *Maeve in America: Essays by a Girl from Somewhere Else*. New York: Penguin Random House, 2018.

Hill, Andrew and John Walton. *A Survey of the Old Testament*. Grand Rapids: Zondervan, 2009.

Hobbes, Thomas. *Leviathan*. Hackett Publishing, 1994.

Holley, Eugene, Jr. "Wynton Marsalis". *Humanities*, Volume 37. November 4, 2016. https://www.neh.gov/humanities/2016/fall/feature/wynton-marsalis

Jenkins, Stephanie. "Drink it In." From Stephanie Jenkins and Kristin Leigh Kludt's "Blessed, a spiritual practice kit," *Field Guides for the Way*. 2019.

Joseph, Jenny. *Warning: When I am an Old Woman, I Shall Wear Purple*. Bury St. Edmonds, Suffolk, UK: Souvenir Press, 1997.

Junod, Tom. "My Friend Mr. Rogers," *The Atlantic*. December 2019. https://www.theatlantic.com/magazine/archive/2019/12/what-would-mister-rogers-do/600772 (Retrieved December 8, 2019).

Kenyon, Jane. "The Suitor." *Otherwise: New and Selected Poems*. Minneapolis: Graywolf Press, 2007.

King, Stephen. *On Writing*. New York: Scribner, 2000.

Lamott, Anne. *Traveling Mercies*. New York: Anchor Books, 1999.

Lee, Wendy. "People spend more time on mobile devices than TV, firm says," *Los Angeles Times*. June 5, 2019. https://www.latimes.com/business/la-fi-ct-people-spend-more-time-on-mobile-than-tv-20190605-story.html.

Lewis, C. S. *Letters to Malcolm*. New York: HarperCollins, 1991.

Lieberstein, Paul. *The Office*. Season 4, episode 04, "Money." Written and directed by Paul Lieberstein, aired October 18, 2007 on NBC.

Liu, Jonathan. "The 5 Best Toys of All Time." *Wired.* January 31, 2011. https://www.wired.com/2011/01/the-5-best-toys-of-all-time (Retrieved September 9, 2019).

Lundgren, Laura. "Village Poet", *Plugged into the vine.* March 11, 2019. https://servantsofgrace.org/village-poet/

Maslow, Abraham. "A Theory of Human Motivation." *Psychological Review*, 50(4), 370–396. July, 1943.

McCarthy, Erin. "20 Awesome Facts About the Golden Gate Bridge." *Mental Floss.* April 14, 2016. http://mentalfloss.com/article/64379/20-awesome-facts-about-golden-gate-bridge (Retrieved February 22, 2019).

Miller, Claire Cain. "The Relentlessness of Modern Parenting." *The New York Times.* December 25, 2018. https://www.nytimes.com/2018/12/25/upshot/the-relentlessness-of-modern-parenting.html?module=inline (Retrieved February 21, 2019).

Milne, A. A. *The Complete Tales of Winnie-the-Pooh.* New York: Dutton Children's Books, 2016.

Muller, Wayne. *Sabbath: Finding Rest, Renewal, and Delight in Our Busy Lives.* New York: Bantam Books, 1999.

Musk, Elon. Quoted by Matt Pressman in "For Elon Musk, Failure Is Critical to Success." *Tesla News.* January 28, 2020. https://evannex.com/blogs/news/for-elon-musk-failure-is-critical-to-success#:~:text=In%20short%2C%20Musk%20believes%20failure,Elon%20Musk%20accepts%20and%20embraces.

Nancherla, Aparna. Twitter Post. August 27, 2019, 1:01 AM. https://twitter.com/aparnapkin/status/1166576608251142146.

Nicolaus, Paul. "Want to Feel Happier Today? Try Talking to a Stranger." *NPR.* July 26, 2019. https://www.npr.org/sections/health-shots/2019/07/26/744267015/want-to-feel-happier-today-try-talking-to-a-stranger.

Norris, Kathleen. "Luke 14: A Commentary," included in Robert Atwan's *Divine Inspiration: The Life of Jesus in World Poetry*, 239.

O'Connor, Flannery. "The Fiction Writer and His Country." *Mystery and Manners*. New York: Farrar, Straus, and Giroux, 1957.

Oliver, Mary. "Maybe." *New and Selected Poems: Volume One*. Boston: Beacon Press, 1992.

Okoro, Enuma. *Silence and Other Surprising Invitations of Advent*. Nashville: Upper Room, 2012.

Paul, Pamela. "Let Children Get Bored Again." *The New York Times*. February 2, 2019. https://www.nytimes.com/2019/02/02/opinion/ sunday/children-bored.html (Retrieved February 21, 2019).

Perez, Sarah. "U.S. adults now spend nearly six hours per day watching video." *Tech Crunch*. July 31, 2018. https://techcrunch. com/2018/07/31/u-s-adults-now-spend-nearly-6-hours-per-day-watching-video (Retrieved January 5, 2020).

Peterson, Andrew. *Adorning the Dark*. Nashville: B & H Publishing Group, 2019.

Peterson, Eugene. *Tell it Slant*. Grand Rapids: Eerdmans, 2012.

Peterson, Eugene. *Working the Angles: The Shape of Pastoral Integrity*. Grand Rapids: Eerdmans, 1987.

Ray, Julie. "Americans' Stress, Worry and Anger Intensified in 2018." *Gallup*. April 25, 2019. https://news.gallup.com/poll/249098/ americans-stress-worry-anger-intensified-2018.aspx.

Raz, Guy. "Khan Academy: Sal Khan." *How I Built This*. Podcast Audio, September 18, 2020. https://www.npr.org/2020/09/18/914394221/ khan-academy-sal-khan#:~:text=Ethics-,Khan%20 Academy%3A%20Sal%20Khan%20%3A%20How%20I%20Built%20 This%20with%20Guy,math%20homework%20over%20the%20 computer.

Redman, Matthew and Jonas Myrin. "10,000 Reasons," Kingsway Music, 2011.

Rohr, Richard. *Falling Upward*. San Francisco: Jossey-Bass, 2011.

Rowling, J. K. author biography in *Harry Potter and the Goblet of Fire*. New York: Scholastic, 2000.

Rubin, Judith ed. "Theme Index, Museum Index 2017." *The Global Attractions Attendance Report*. Themed Entertainment Association. http://www.teaconnect.org/images/files/TEA_268_653730_180517.pdf (Retrieved February 20, 2020).

Sandburg, Carl. "Fog". *Selected Poems*. Boston: Mariner Books, 1996.

Satara, Alyssa. "Elon Musk Says That Key to Success is Failure, Here's Why." *Noteworthy – The Journal Blog*. August 15, 2019.

Seah, Jean Elizabeth. "Taking Back Sundays for Holy Leisure." *Aleteia*. October 15, 2017. https://aleteia.org/2017/10/15/taking-back-sundays-for-the-sake-of-holy-leisure. (Retrieved February 10, 2020).

Shellnutt, Kate. "If You Give a Tsunami Survivor a Crayon." *Christianity Today*. November 27, 2018. https://www.christianitytoday.com/ct/2018/december/indonesia-tsunami-relief-children-safe-spaces-sulawesi.html (Retrieved October 5, 2019).

Simon, Paul. "Improvisation is too good to leave to chance." *The Observer*. Quoted in *Oxford Essential Quotations: Fourth Edition*. Oxford: Oxford University Press, 2016.

Smucker, Shawn. "Dad, I Love This Day." March 17, 2020. http://shawnsmucker.com/2020/03/dad-i-love-this-day (Retrieved October 4, 2020).

Stetzer, Ed. "Brand New Research: Mother's Day is a Top Non-Religious Holiday for Church Attendance." *Christianity Today*. May 11, 2012. https://www.christianitytoday.com/edstetzer/2012/may/brand-new-research-mothers-day-is-top-non-religious.html.

Taylor, Bill. "How Coca-Cola, Netflix, and Amazon Learn from Failure." *Harvard Business Review*. November 10, 2017. https://hbr.org/2017/11/how-coca-cola-netflix-and-amazon-learn-from-failure (Retrieved February 10, 2020).

Tugwell, Simon. "Prayer." As quoted in *A Guide to Prayer for Ministers and Other Servants*. Nashville: Upper Room, 1983.

Tugwell, Simon. *Prayer: Living with God.* Dublin: Veritas, 1975.

United States Bureau of Labor Statistics. "Consumer Expenditures 2018." https://www.bls.gov/news.release/cesan.nro.htm (Retrieved February 20, 2020).

United States Department of Labor, Bureau of Labor Statistics. "American Time Use Survey—2019 Results." https://www.bls.gov/news.release/atus.nro.htm (Retrieved December 8, 2019).

Vanderkam, Laura. "Working from home poses serious danger for employers and employees alike." *Fortune.* August 2, 2020. https://fortune.com/2020/08/02/coronavirus-remote-work-home-burnout.

Walton, John H. *Chronological and Background Charts of the Old Testament.* Grand Rapids: Zondervan, 1994.

Warren, Tish Harrison. *Liturgy of the Ordinary: Sacred Practices in Everyday Life.* Downers Grove, IL: InterVarsity Press, 2016.

Washington, Booker T. *The Story of My Life in Work.* New Casa, 2020.

Wells, H. G. as quoted in "Will Bicycles Save the Human Race?" by Bogdan Hobal. *New York Public Library Blog.* March 14, 2014. https://www.nypl.org/blog/2014/03/14/will-bicycles-save-human-race.

Williams, Tennessee. *Camino Real.* New York: New Direction, 2008.

Wollstonecraft, Mary. *Mary. A Fiction.* Horse's Mouth, 2019.

Woofenden, Anna. *This is God's Table: Finding Church Beyond the Walls.* Harrisonburg, VA: Herald Press, 2020.

OTHER BOOKS BY COURTNEY ELLIS

Uncluttered: Free Your Space, Free Your Schedule, Free Your Soul

Too much stuff. Too many activities. Too much exhaustion. Too much stress. How can we sift through the busyness, the mess, and the stress to uncover the abundant life God offers?

In *Uncluttered*, Courtney Ellis shares her journey from a life of stress, stuff, and burnout to one of peace, space, and fulfillment. You'll learn tips for paring down your possessions, simplifying your schedule, and practicing the ancient art of Sabbath.

ISBN: 9781628627916

Almost Holy Mama: Life-Giving Spiritual Practices for Weary Parents

With the honesty of a close friend, the hilarity of a late-night comic, and the humility of a mom up to her eyeballs in diapers and dishes, Courtney Ellis invites you on a journey to draw closer to God amid the joyful, mundane, exhausting days of young parenthood.

In *Almost Holy Mama*, Courtney chronicles her quest to discover an answer to her most pressing question: Can God use the crucible of parenthood to grow us in virtue?

ISBN: 9781628627909

Available at www.HendricksonRose.com